THE AMAZING
SCREW-ON
HEAD

and Other Curious Object

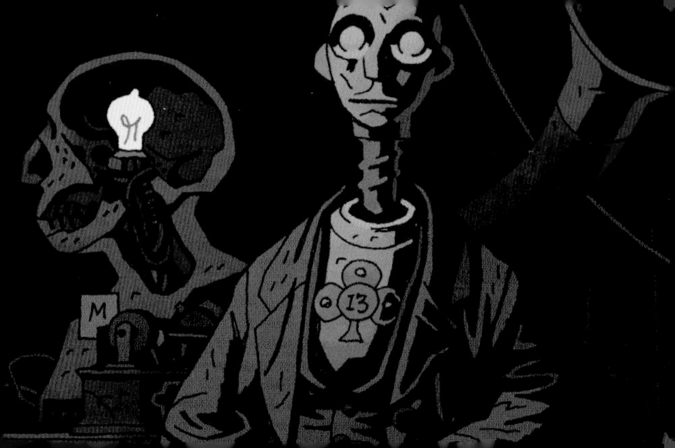
M
13

THE AMAZING SCREW-ON HEAD™

and Other Curious Objects

by MIKE MIGNOLA

"The Magician and the Snake"
by KATIE MIGNOLA and
MIKE MIGNOLA

colors by
DAVE STEWART

letters by
CLEM ROBINS & PAT BROSSEAU

editor SCOTT ALLIE
associate editor SAMANTHA ROBERTSON
assistant editor DANIEL CHABON
collection designer AMY ARENDTS
publisher MIKE RICHARDSON

DARK HORSE BOOKS®

Published by
Dark Horse Books
A division of
Dark Horse Comics, Inc.
10956 SE Main Street
Milwaukie, OR 97222

First Edition: August 2010
ISBN: 978-1-59582-501-8

3 5 7 9 10 8 6 4 2
Printed at 1010 Printing International, Ltd., Guangdong Province, China

Image on the facing page is available from the United States Library of Congress's
Prints and Photographs Division under the digital ID cph.3a53289

This book collects *The Amazing Screw-On Head* comic book, the story "The Magician
and the Snake" from *Dark Horse Maverick: Happy Endings*, published by
Dark Horse Comics, and several new stories.

For my wife, my daughter, and former
U.S. President Abraham Lincoln.

PART ONE

THE AMAZING SCREW-ON HEAD

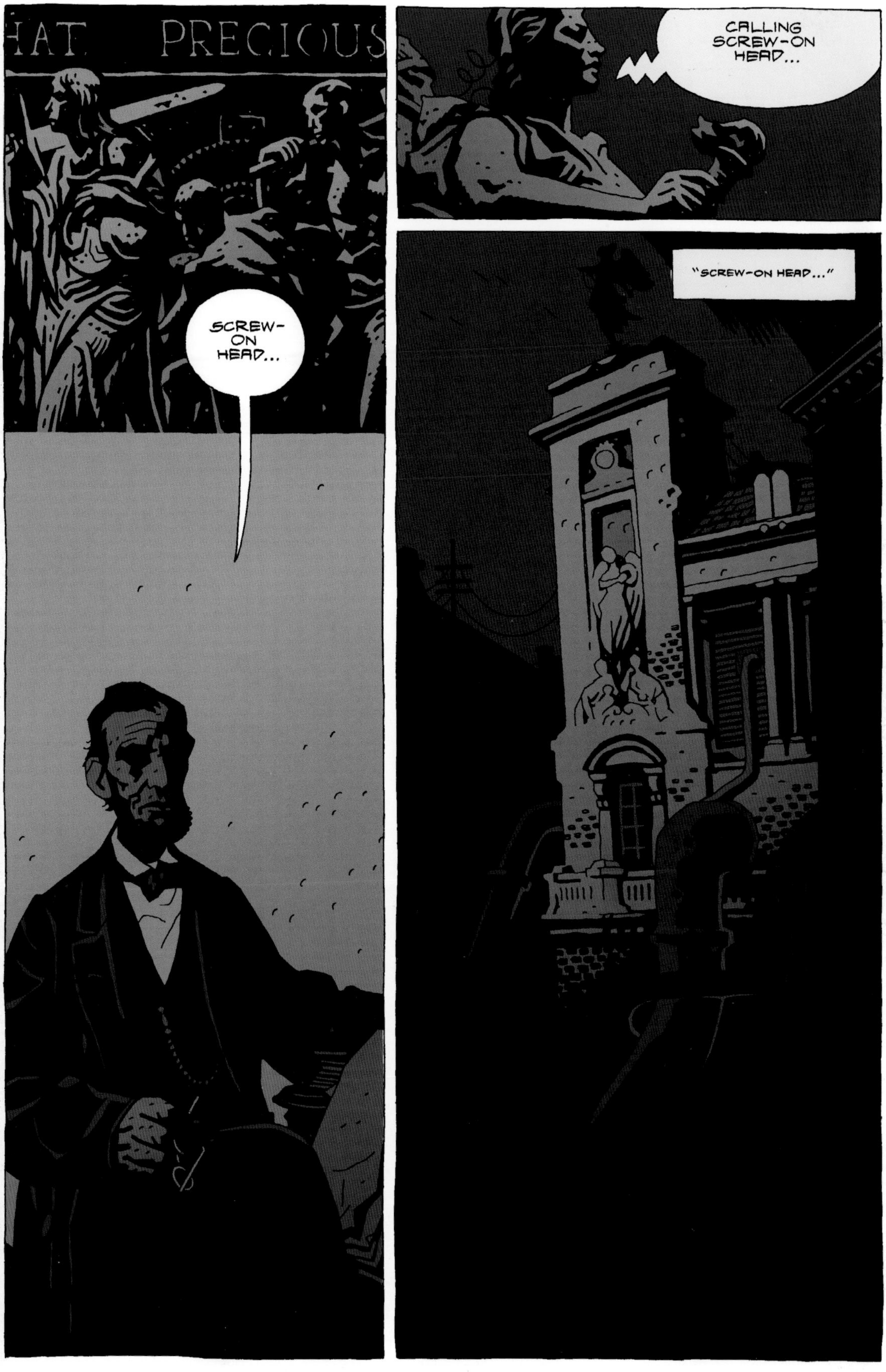
HAT PRECIOUS
SCREW-ON HEAD...
CALLING SCREW-ON HEAD...
"SCREW-ON HEAD..."

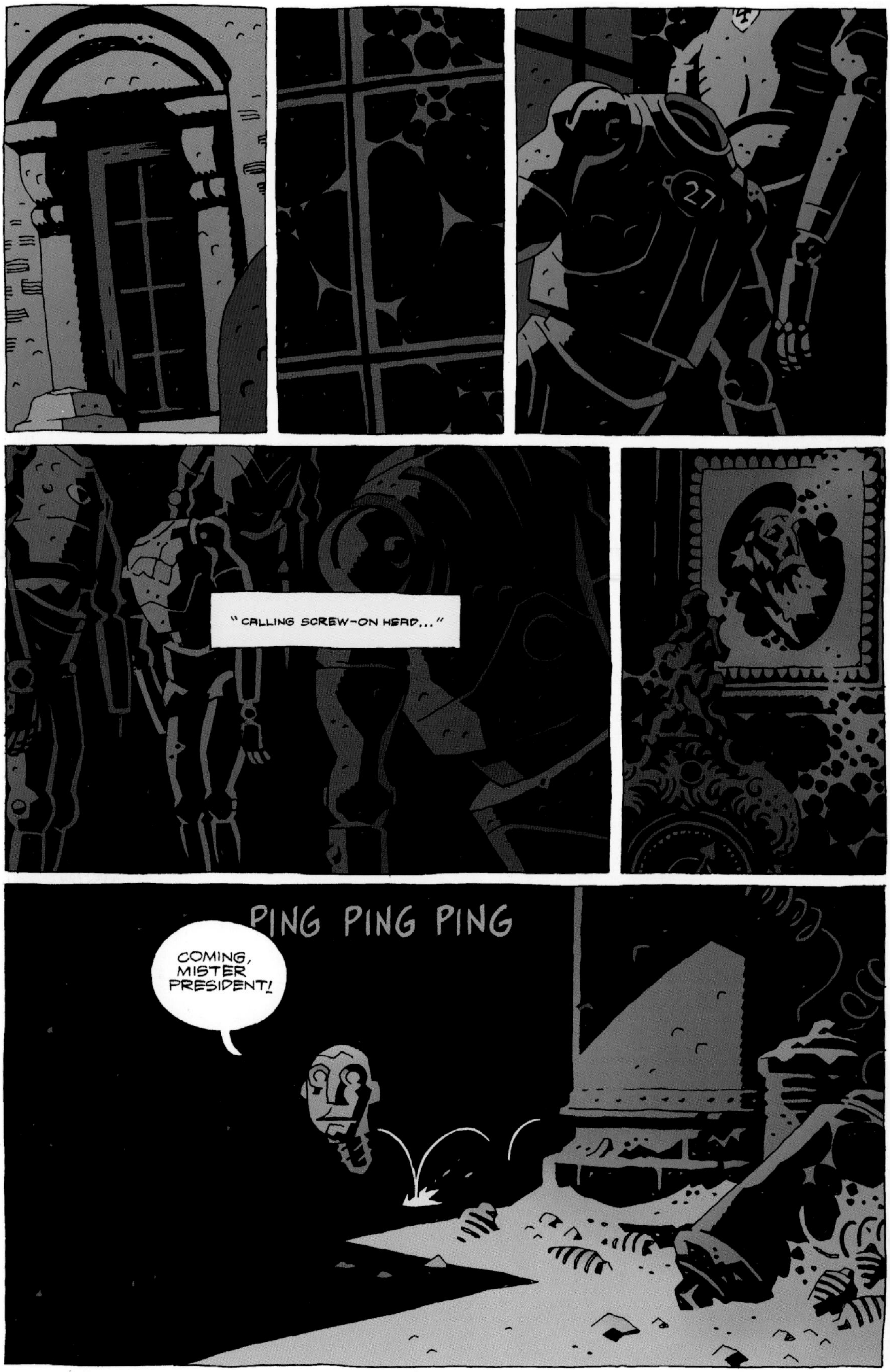
"CALLING SCREW-ON HEAD..."
PING PING PING
COMING, MISTER PRESIDENT!

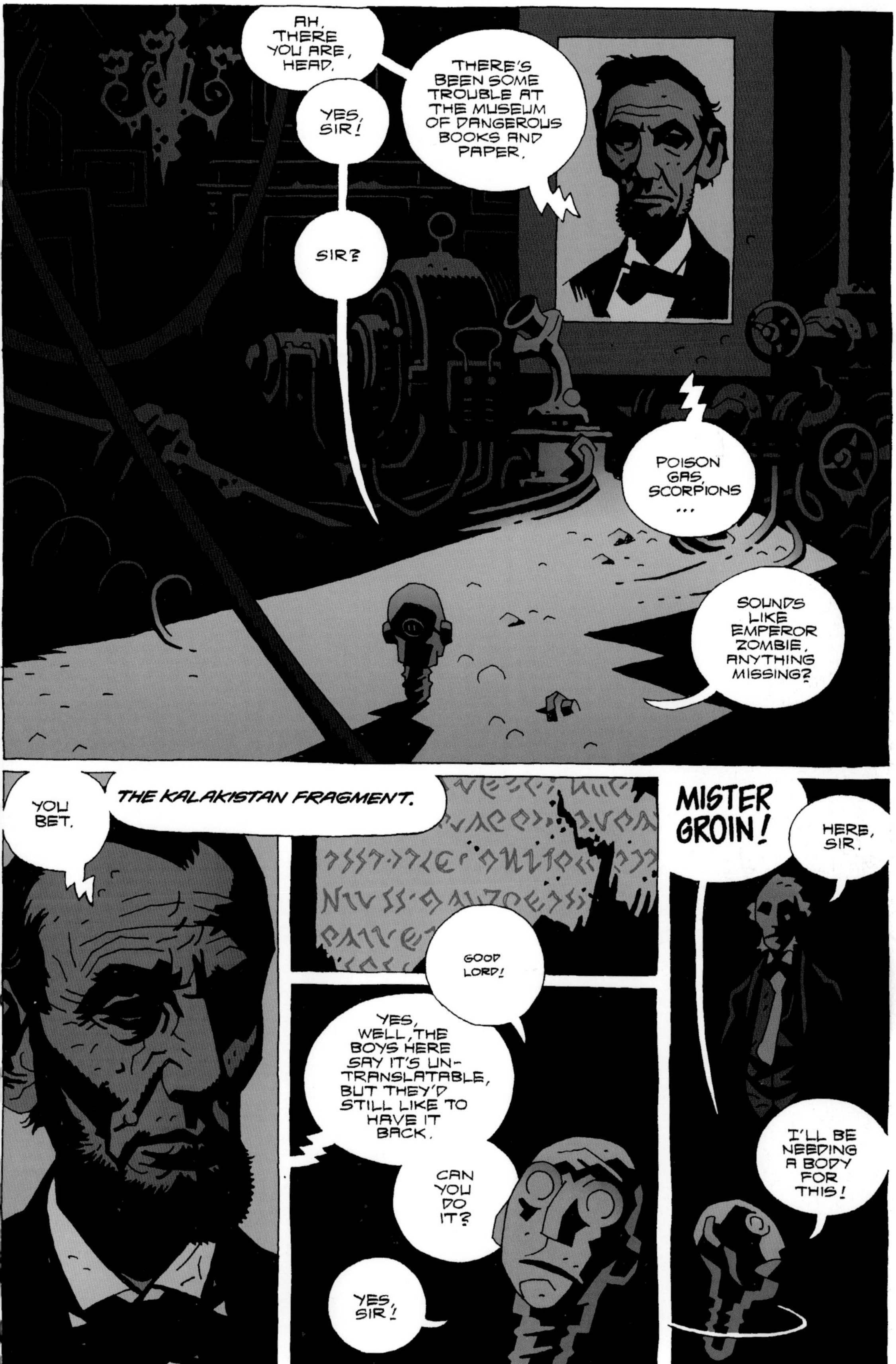
AH, THERE YOU ARE, HEAD.
THERE'S BEEN SOME TROUBLE AT THE MUSEUM OF DANGEROUS BOOKS AND PAPER.
YES, SIR!
SIR?
POISON GAS, SCORPIONS ...
SOUNDS LIKE EMPEROR ZOMBIE. ANYTHING MISSING?
YOU BET.
THE KALAKISTAN FRAGMENT.
GOOD LORD!
YES, WELL, THE BOYS HERE SAY IT'S UN-TRANSLATABLE, BUT THEY'D STILL LIKE TO HAVE IT BACK.
CAN YOU DO IT?
YES, SIR!
MISTER GROIN!
HERE, SIR.
I'LL BE NEEDING A BODY FOR THIS!

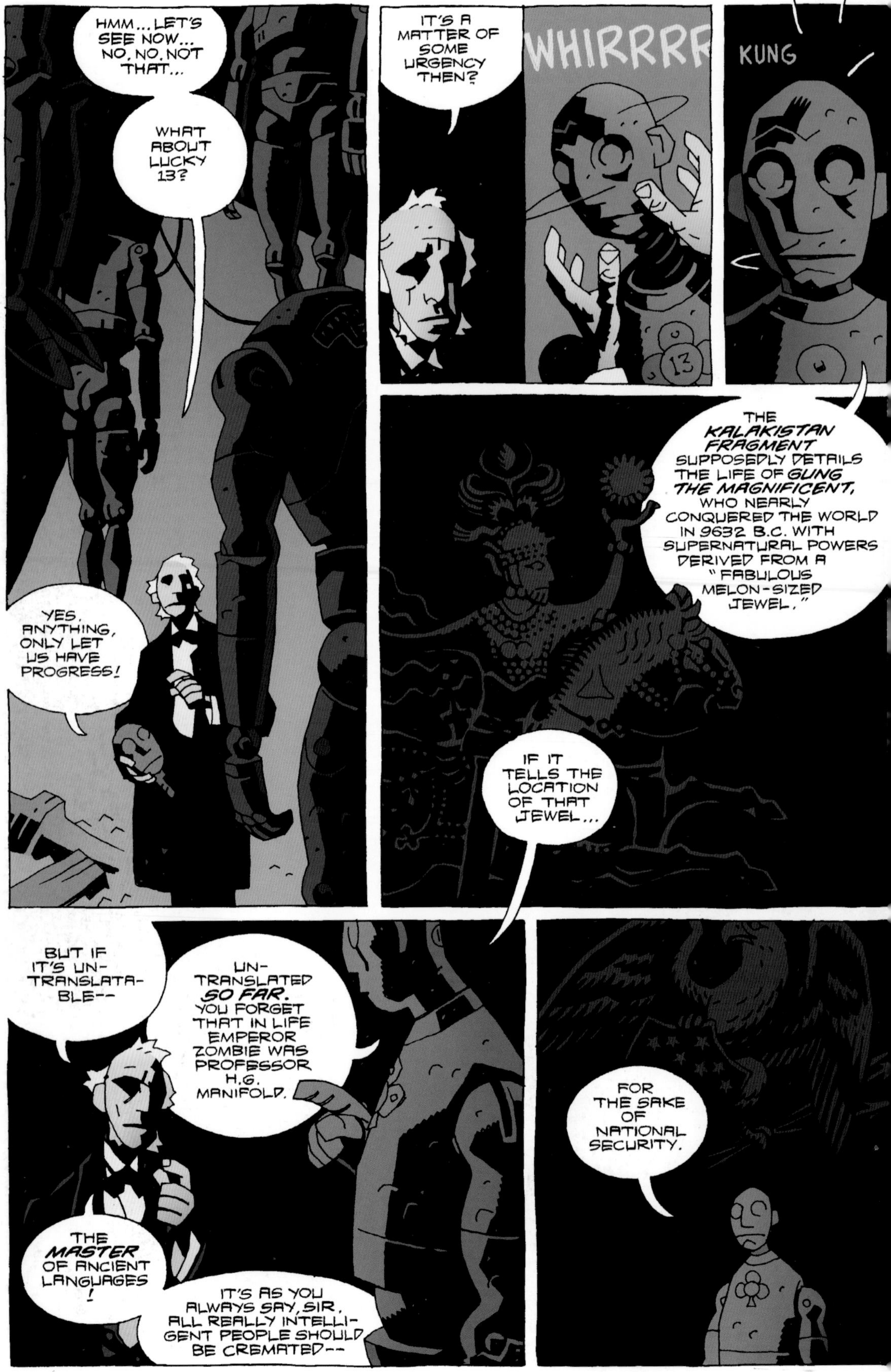
HMM... LET'S SEE NOW... NO, NO, NOT THAT...
WHAT ABOUT LUCKY 13?
YES. ANYTHING, ONLY LET US HAVE PROGRESS!
IT'S A MATTER OF SOME URGENCY THEN?
WHIRRRR
KUNG
THE KALAKISTAN FRAGMENT SUPPOSEDLY DETAILS THE LIFE OF GUNG THE MAGNIFICENT, WHO NEARLY CONQUERED THE WORLD IN 9632 B.C. WITH SUPERNATURAL POWERS DERIVED FROM A "FABULOUS MELON-SIZED JEWEL."
IF IT TELLS THE LOCATION OF THAT JEWEL...
BUT IF IT'S UN-TRANSLATA-BLE--
UN-TRANSLATED SO FAR. YOU FORGET THAT IN LIFE EMPEROR ZOMBIE WAS PROFESSOR H.G. MANIFOLD.
THE MASTER OF ANCIENT LANGUAGES!
IT'S AS YOU ALWAYS SAY, SIR, ALL REALLY INTELLI-GENT PEOPLE SHOULD BE CREMATED--
FOR THE SAKE OF NATIONAL SECURITY.

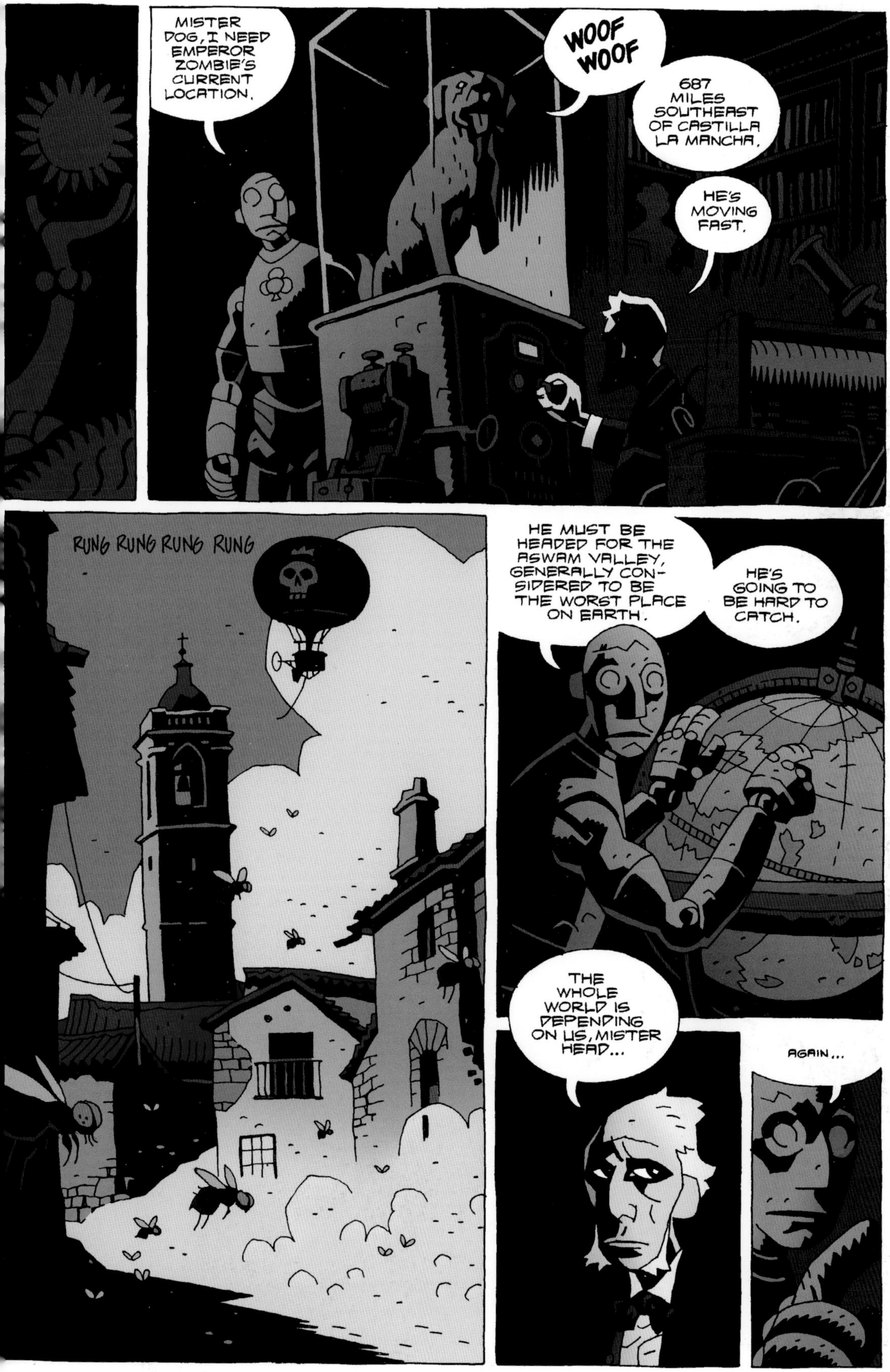
MISTER DOG, I NEED EMPEROR ZOMBIE'S CURRENT LOCATION.
WOOF WOOF
687 MILES SOUTHEAST OF CASTILLA LA MANCHA.
HE'S MOVING FAST.
RUNG RUNG RUNG RUNG
HE MUST BE HEADED FOR THE ASWAM VALLEY, GENERALLY CON-SIDERED TO BE THE WORST PLACE ON EARTH.
HE'S GOING TO BE HARD TO CATCH.
THE WHOLE WORLD IS DEPENDING ON US, MISTER HEAD...
AGAIN...

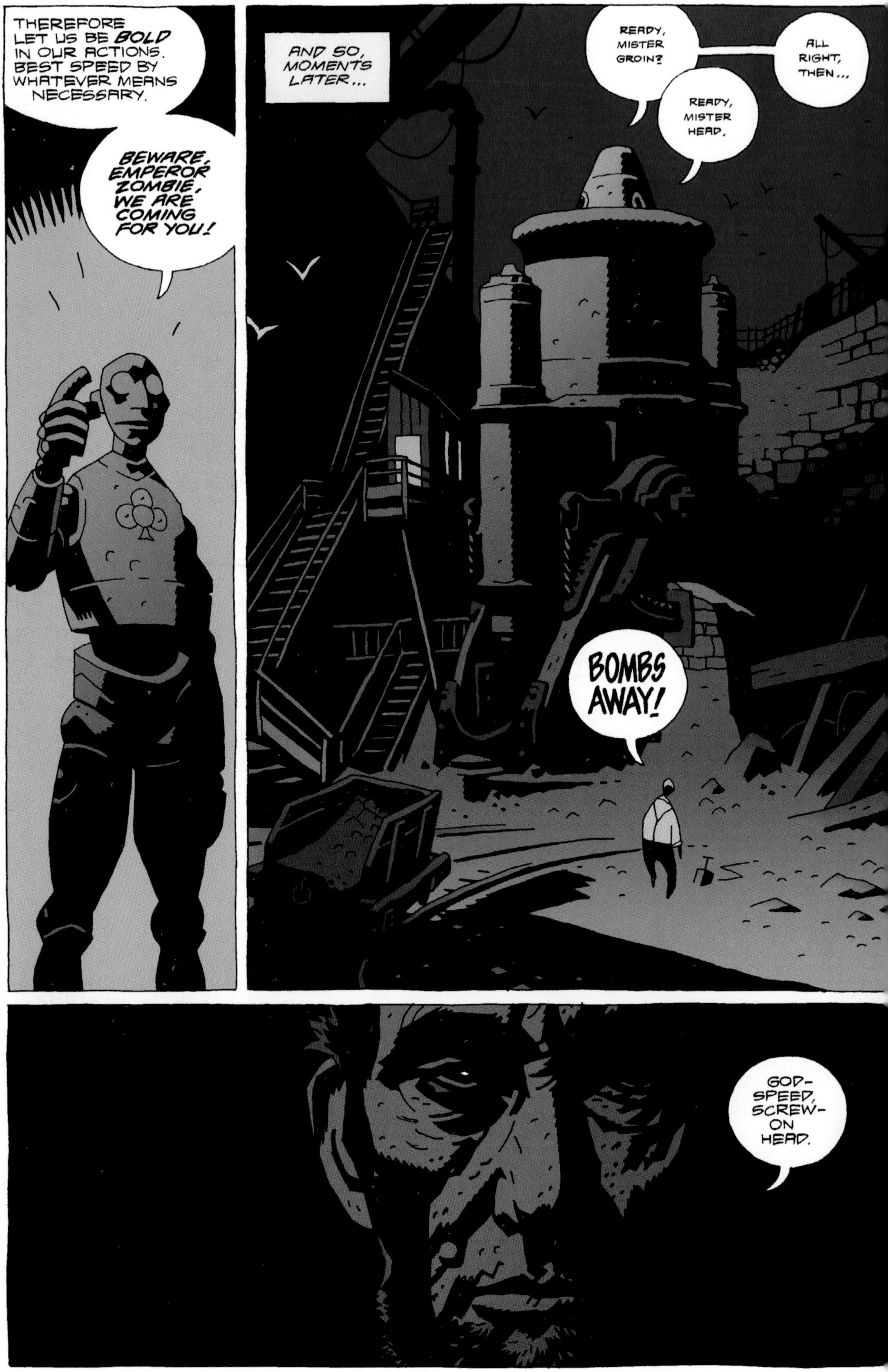
THEREFORE LET US BE BOLD IN OUR ACTIONS. BEST SPEED BY WHATEVER MEANS NECESSARY.
BEWARE, EMPEROR ZOMBIE, WE ARE COMING FOR YOU!
AND SO, MOMENTS LATER...
READY, MISTER GROIN?
READY, MISTER HEAD.
ALL RIGHT, THEN...
BOMBS AWAY!
GOD-SPEED, SCREW-ON HEAD.

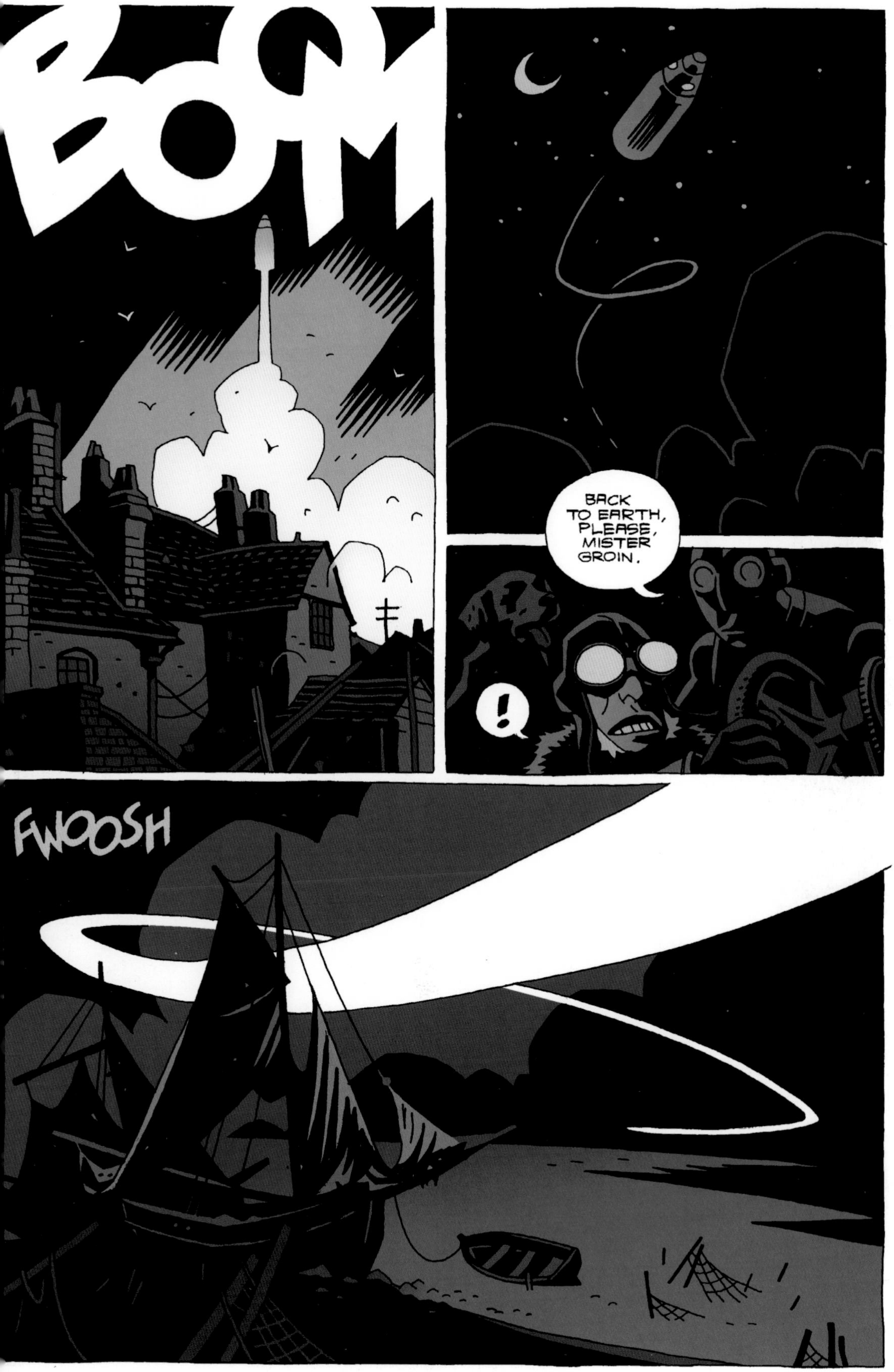
BOOM
BACK TO EARTH, PLEASE, MISTER GROIN.
!
FWOOSH

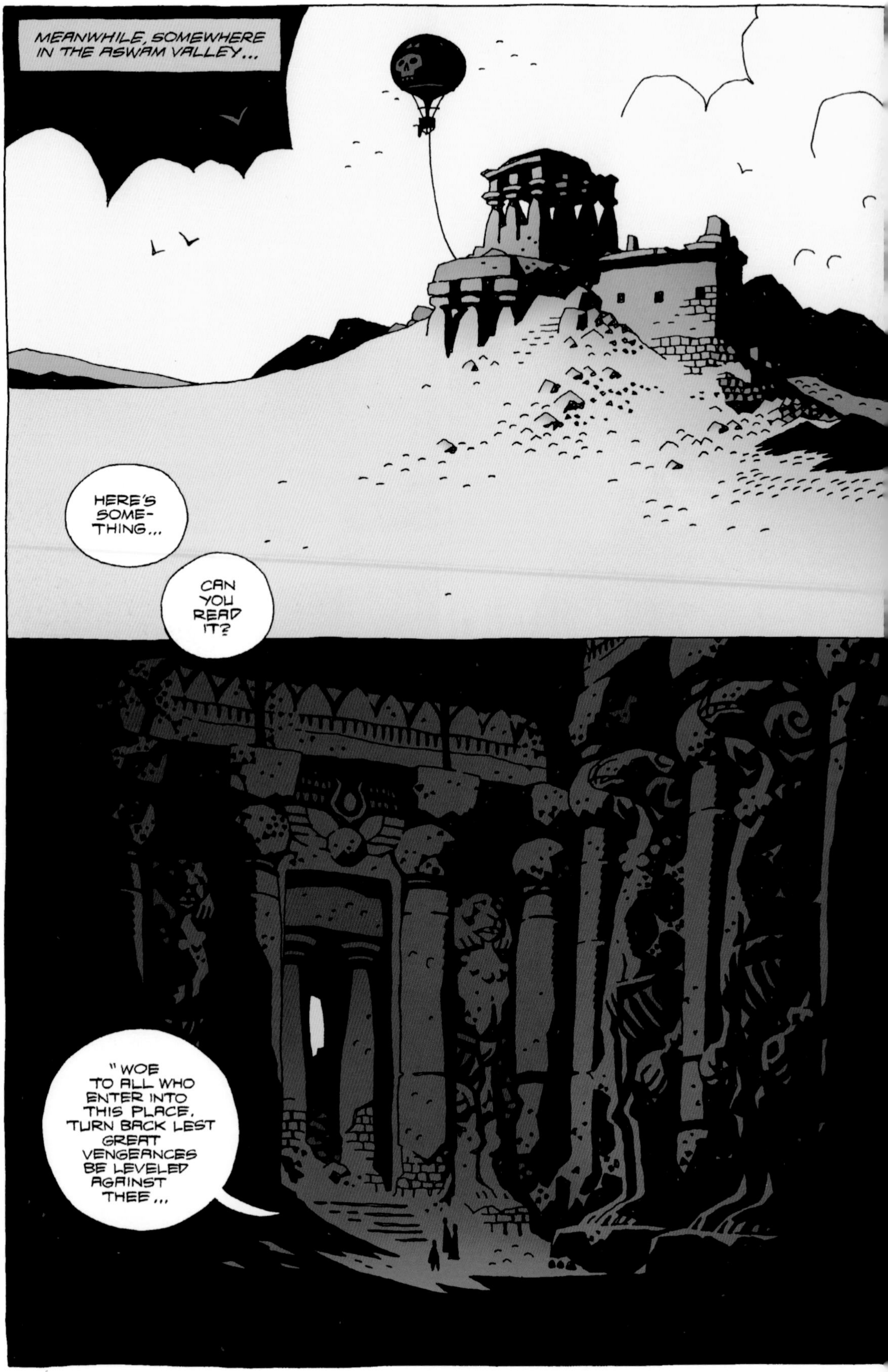
MEANWHILE, SOMEWHERE IN THE ASWAM VALLEY...
HERE'S SOME-THING...
CAN YOU READ IT?
"WOE TO ALL WHO ENTER INTO THIS PLACE. TURN BACK LEST GREAT VENGEANCES BE LEVELED AGAINST THEE...

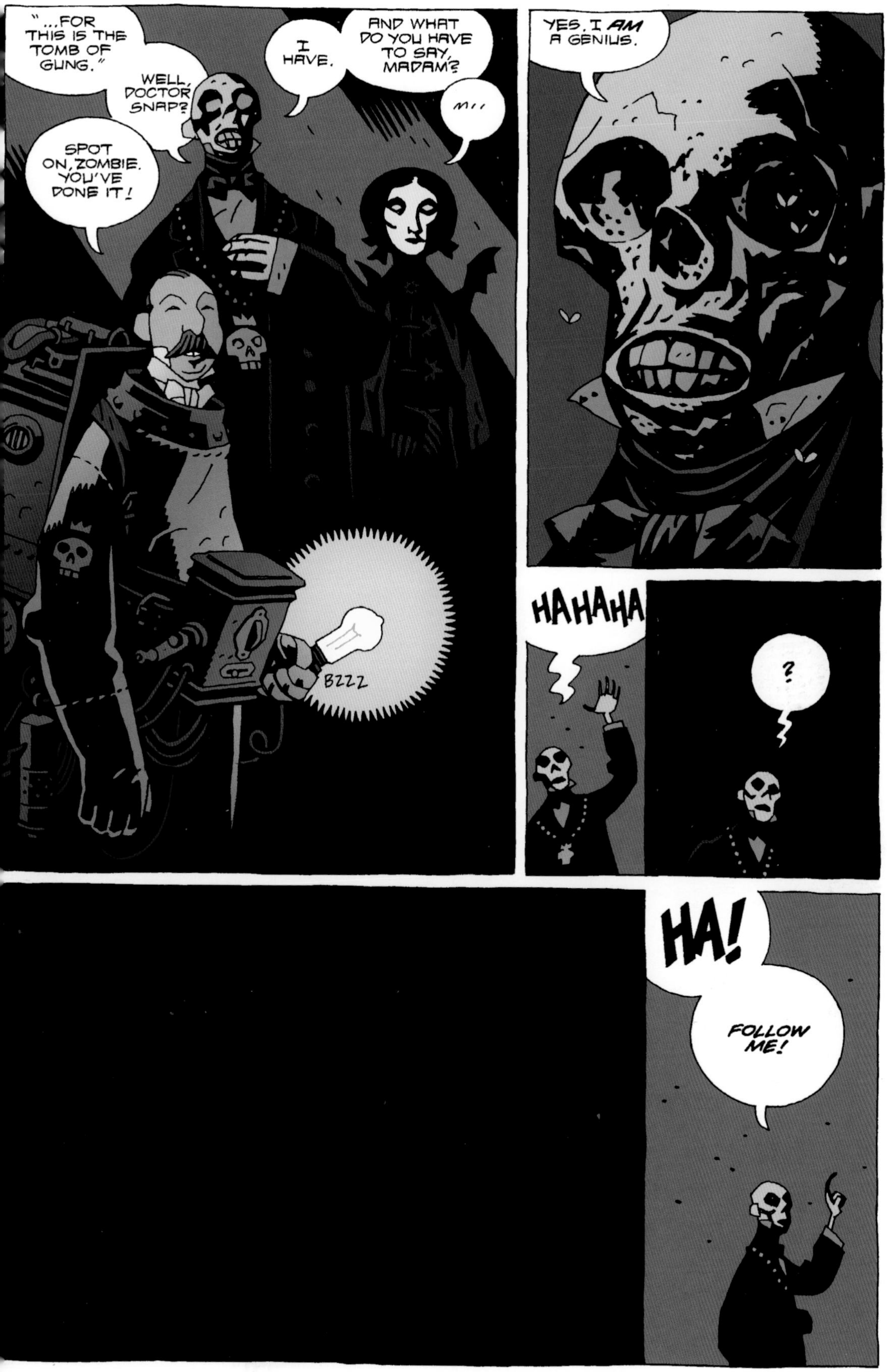
"...FOR THIS IS THE TOMB OF GUNG."
WELL, DOCTOR SNAP?
SPOT ON, ZOMBIE. YOU'VE DONE IT!
I HAVE.
AND WHAT DO YOU HAVE TO SAY, MADAM?
M!!
BZZZ
YES, I AM A GENIUS.
HAHAHA
?
HA!
FOLLOW ME!

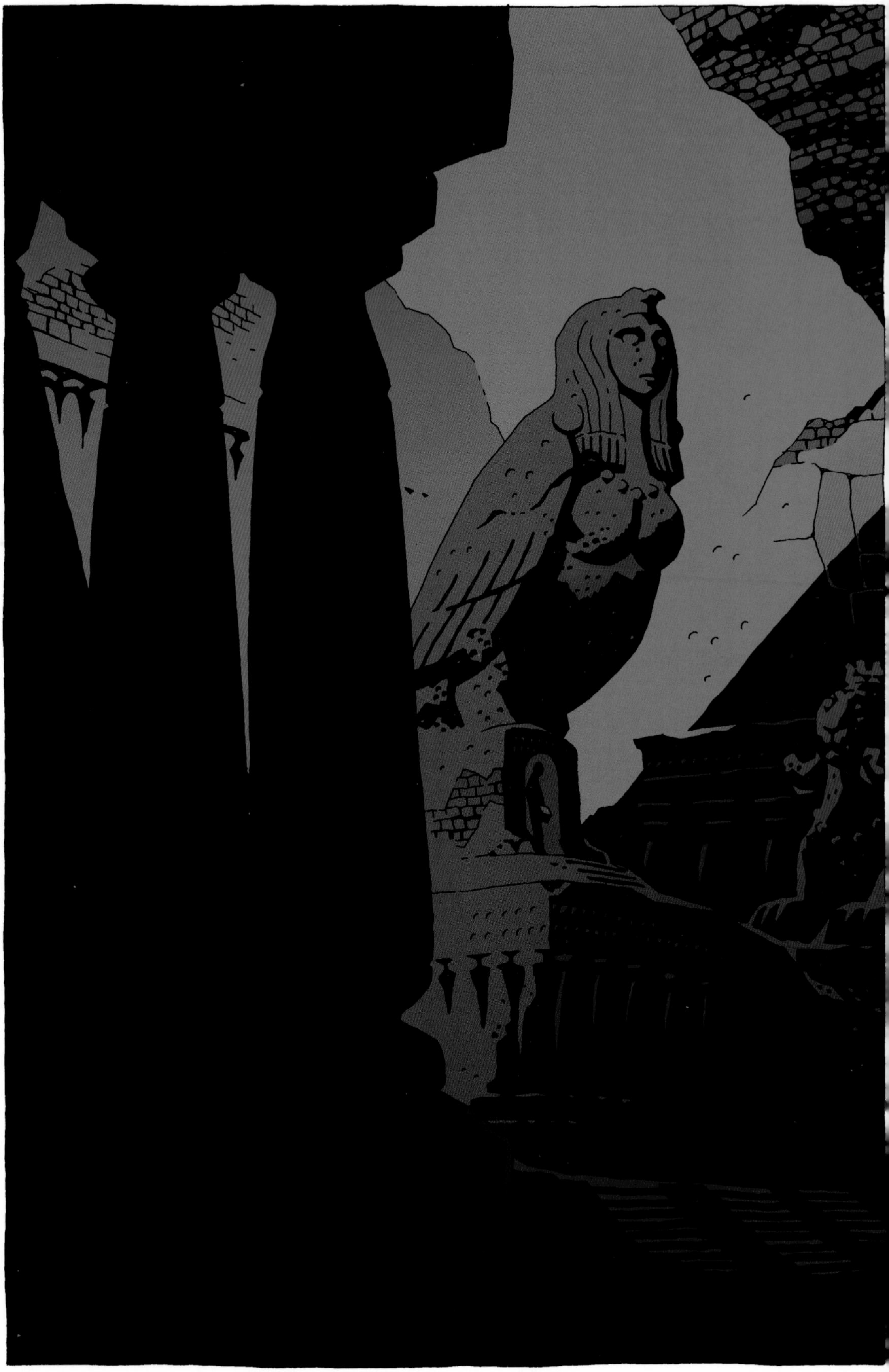

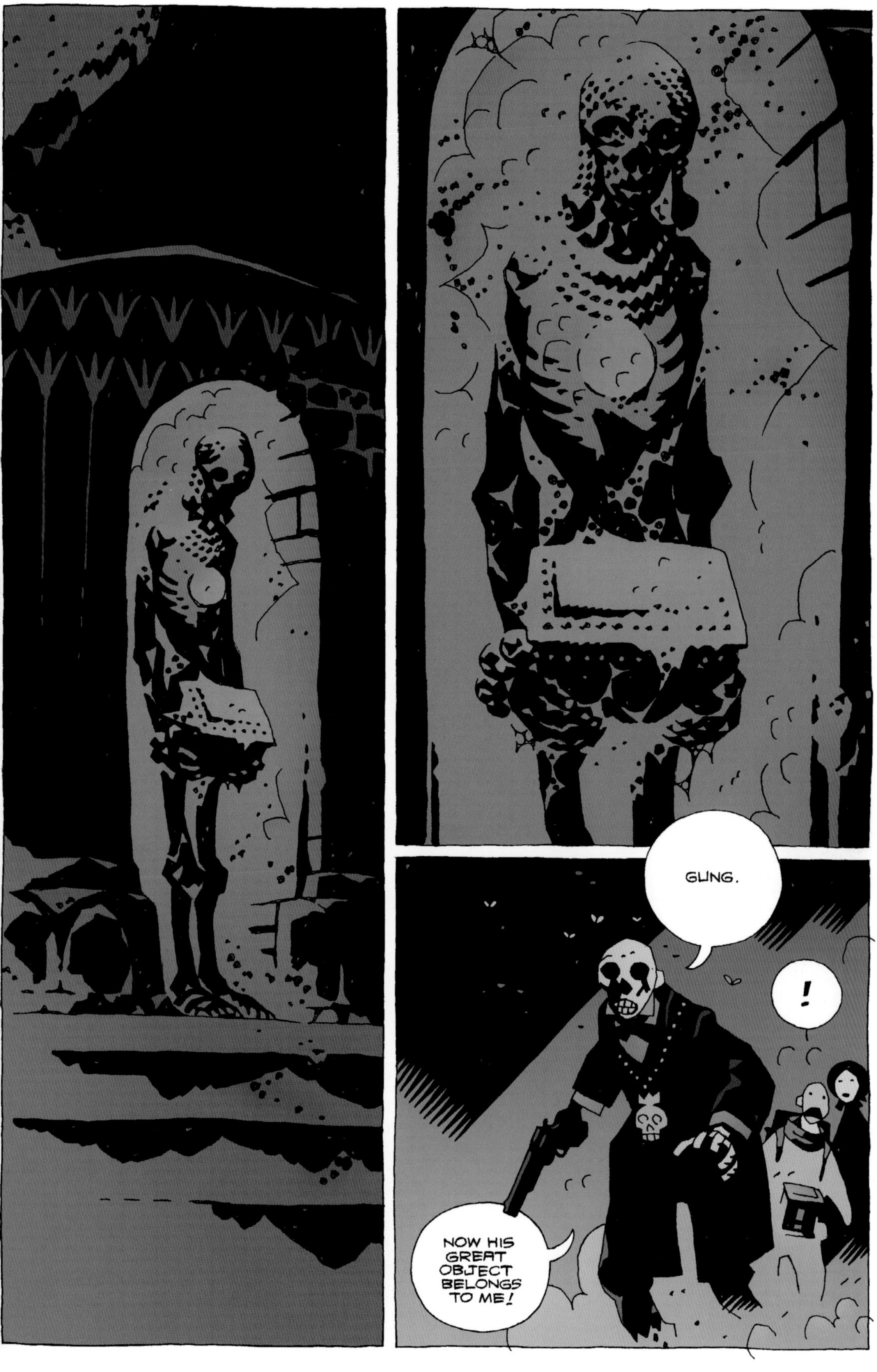
GUNG.
!
NOW HIS GREAT OBJECT BELONGS TO ME!

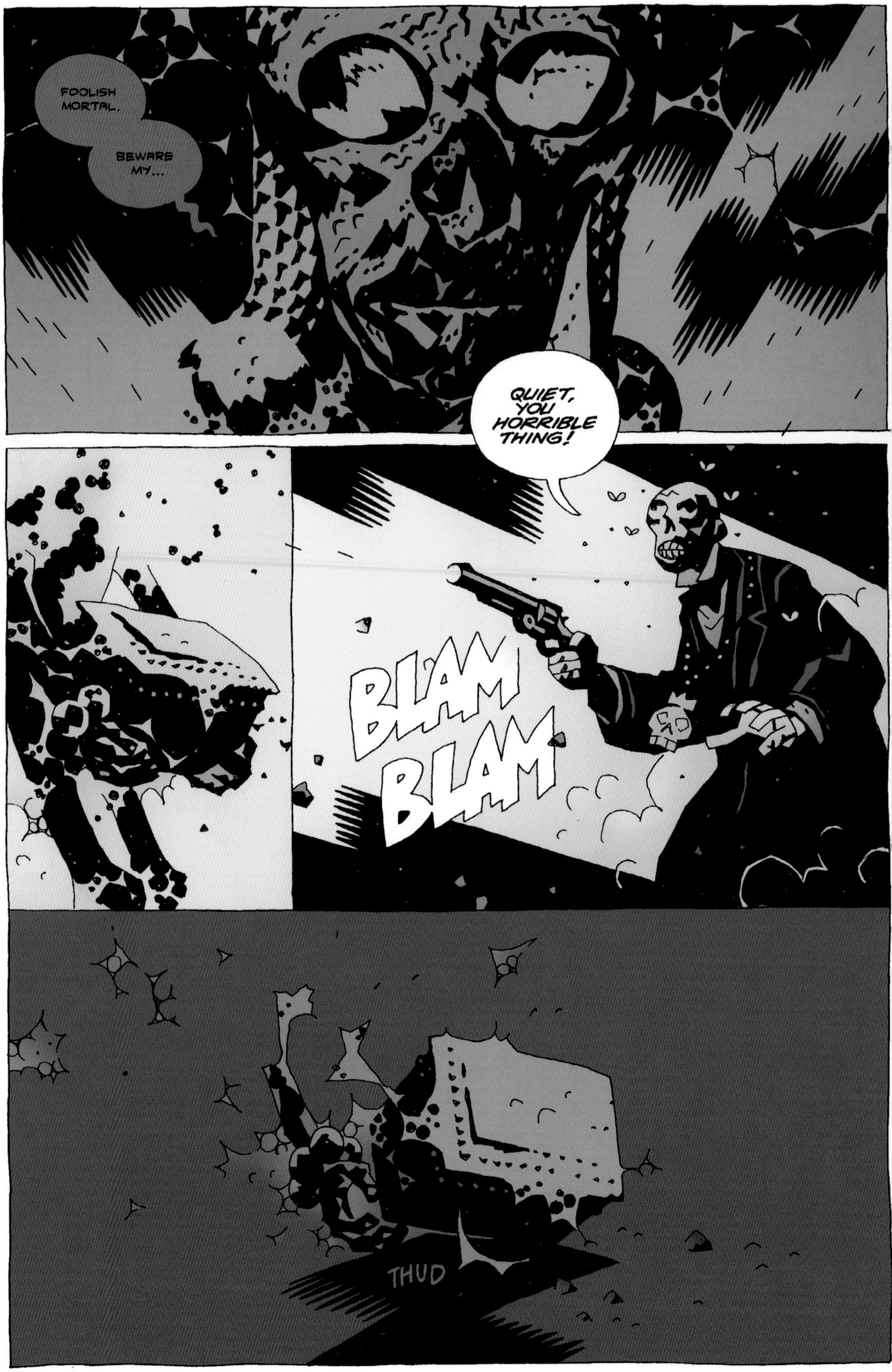
FOOLISH MORTAL.
BEWARE MY...
QUIET, YOU HORRIBLE THING!
BLAM BLAM
THUD

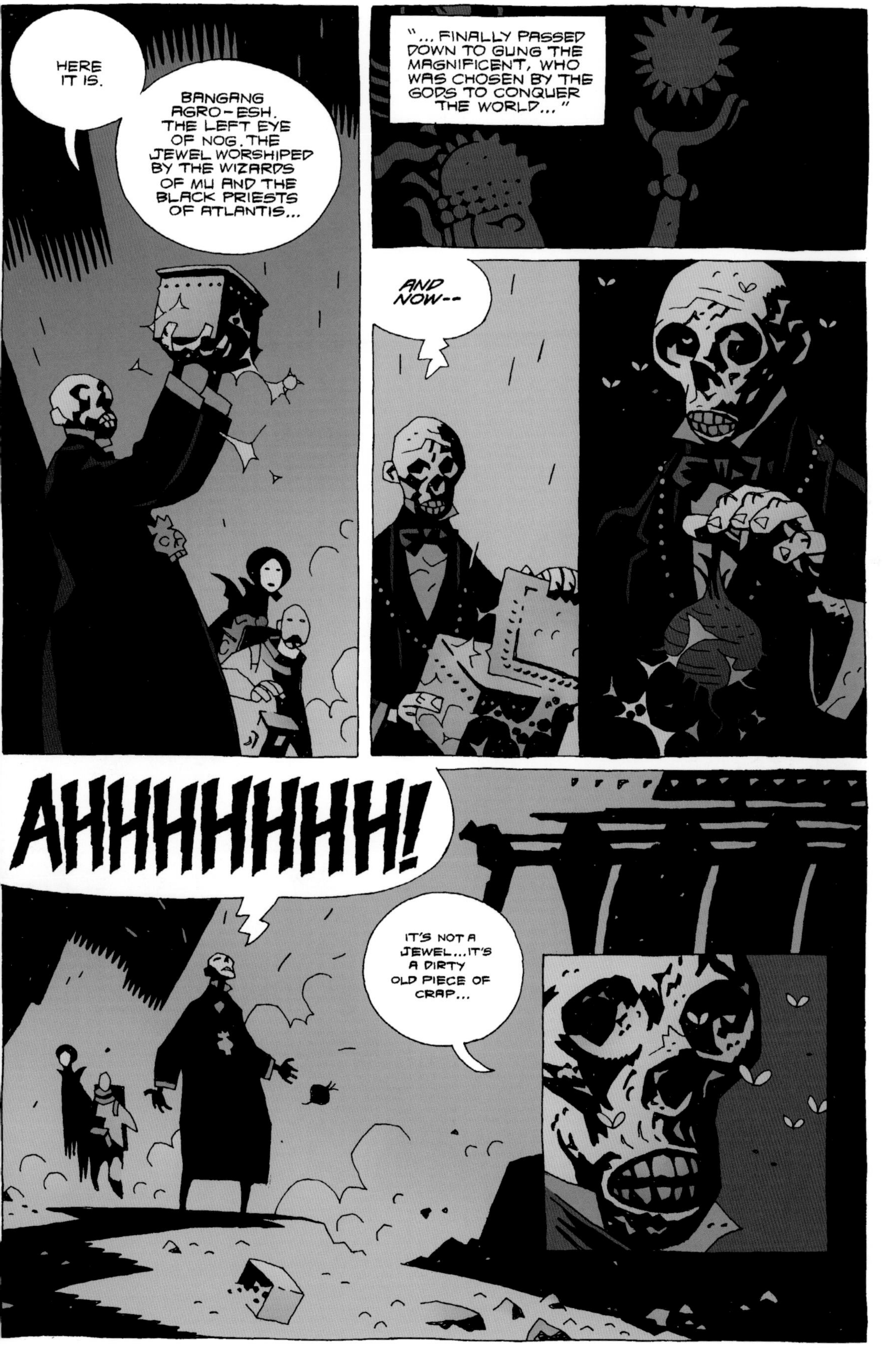

HERE IT IS.
BANGANG AGRO-ESH. THE LEFT EYE OF NOG. THE JEWEL WORSHIPED BY THE WIZARDS OF MU AND THE BLACK PRIESTS OF ATLANTIS...
"... FINALLY PASSED DOWN TO GUNG THE MAGNIFICENT, WHO WAS CHOSEN BY THE GODS TO CONQUER THE WORLD..."
AND NOW--
AHHHHHHH!
IT'S NOT A JEWEL...IT'S A DIRTY OLD PIECE OF CRAP...

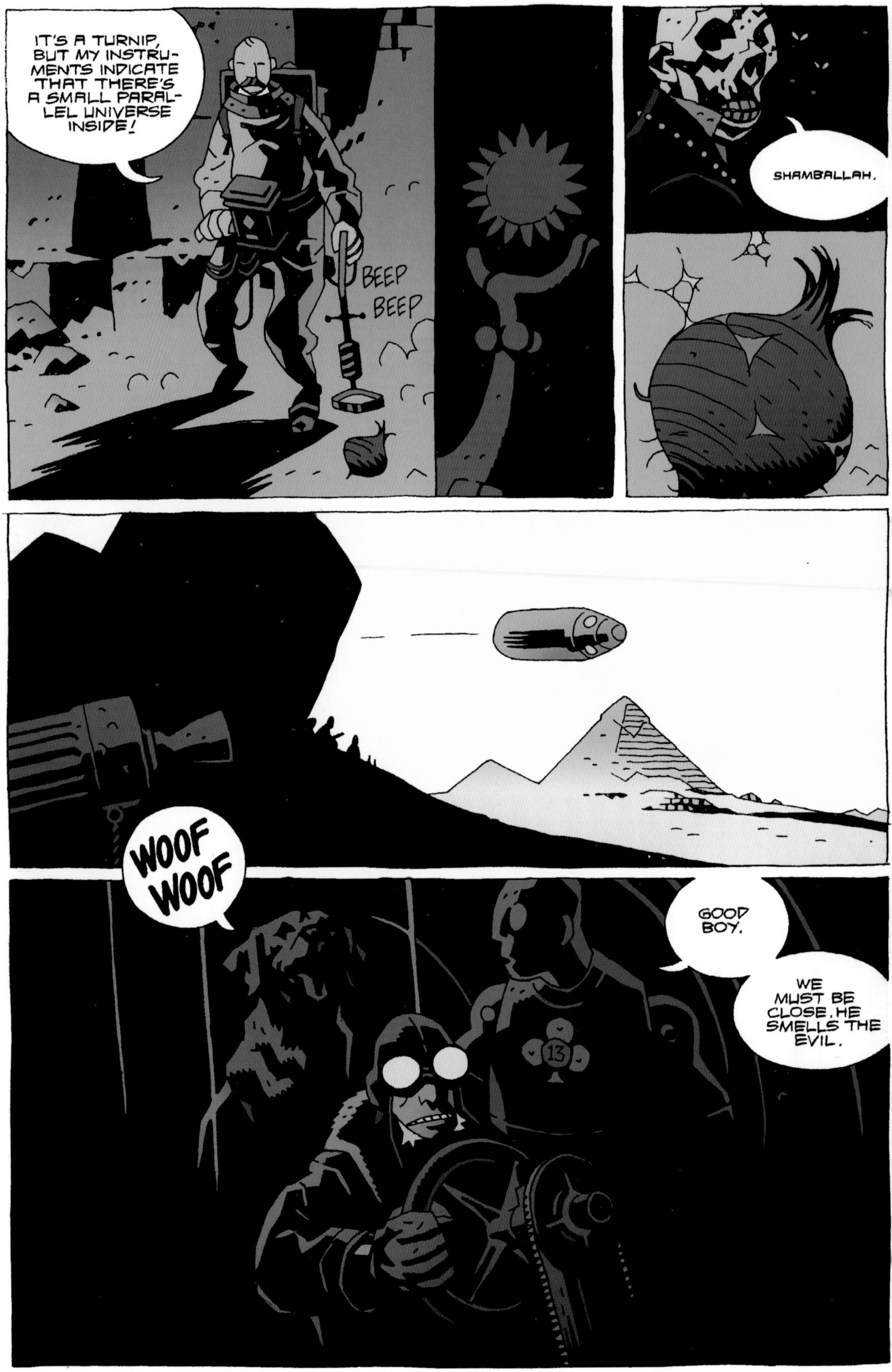
IT'S A TURNIP, BUT MY INSTRUMENTS INDICATE THAT THERE'S A SMALL PARALLEL UNIVERSE INSIDE!
BEEP
BEEP
SHAMBALLAH.
WOOF WOOF
GOOD BOY.
WE MUST BE CLOSE. HE SMELLS THE EVIL.

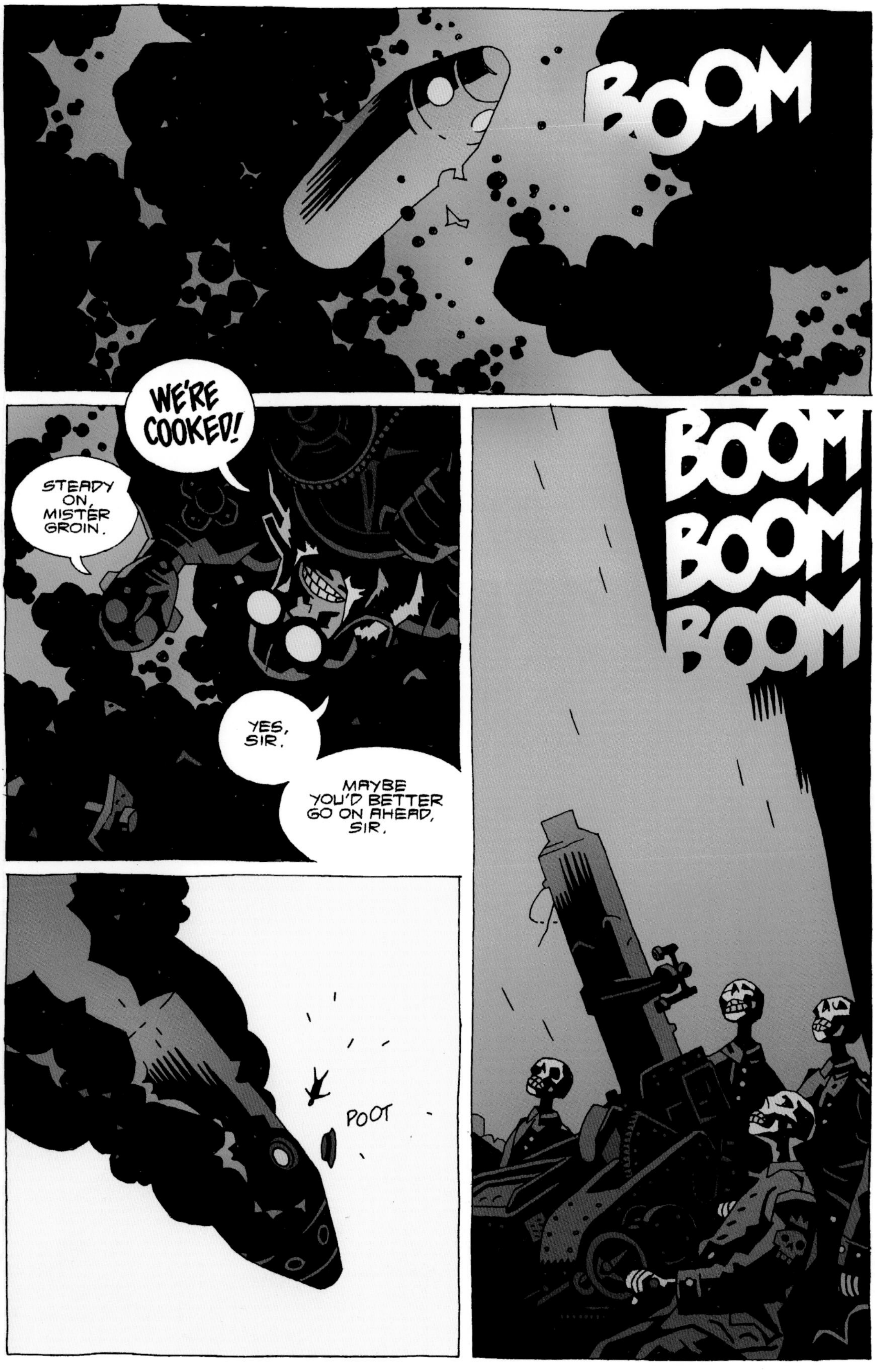
BOOM
WE'RE COOKED!
STEADY ON, MISTER GROIN.
YES, SIR.
MAYBE YOU'D BETTER GO ON AHEAD, SIR.
BOOM BOOM BOOM BOOM
POOT

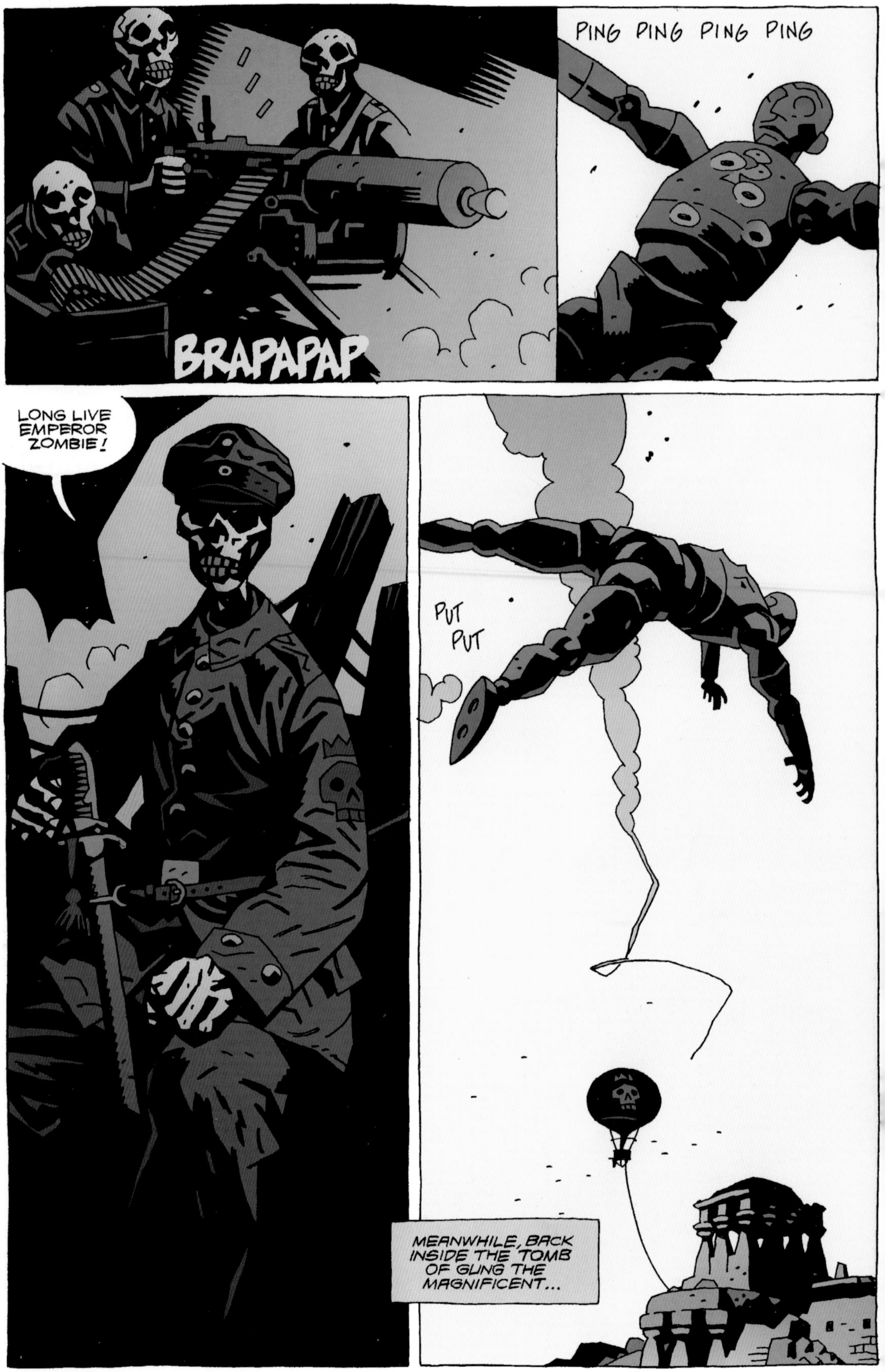
BRAPAPAP
PING PING PING PING
LONG LIVE EMPEROR ZOMBIE!
PUT PUT
MEANWHILE, BACK INSIDE THE TOMB OF GUNG THE MAGNIFICENT...

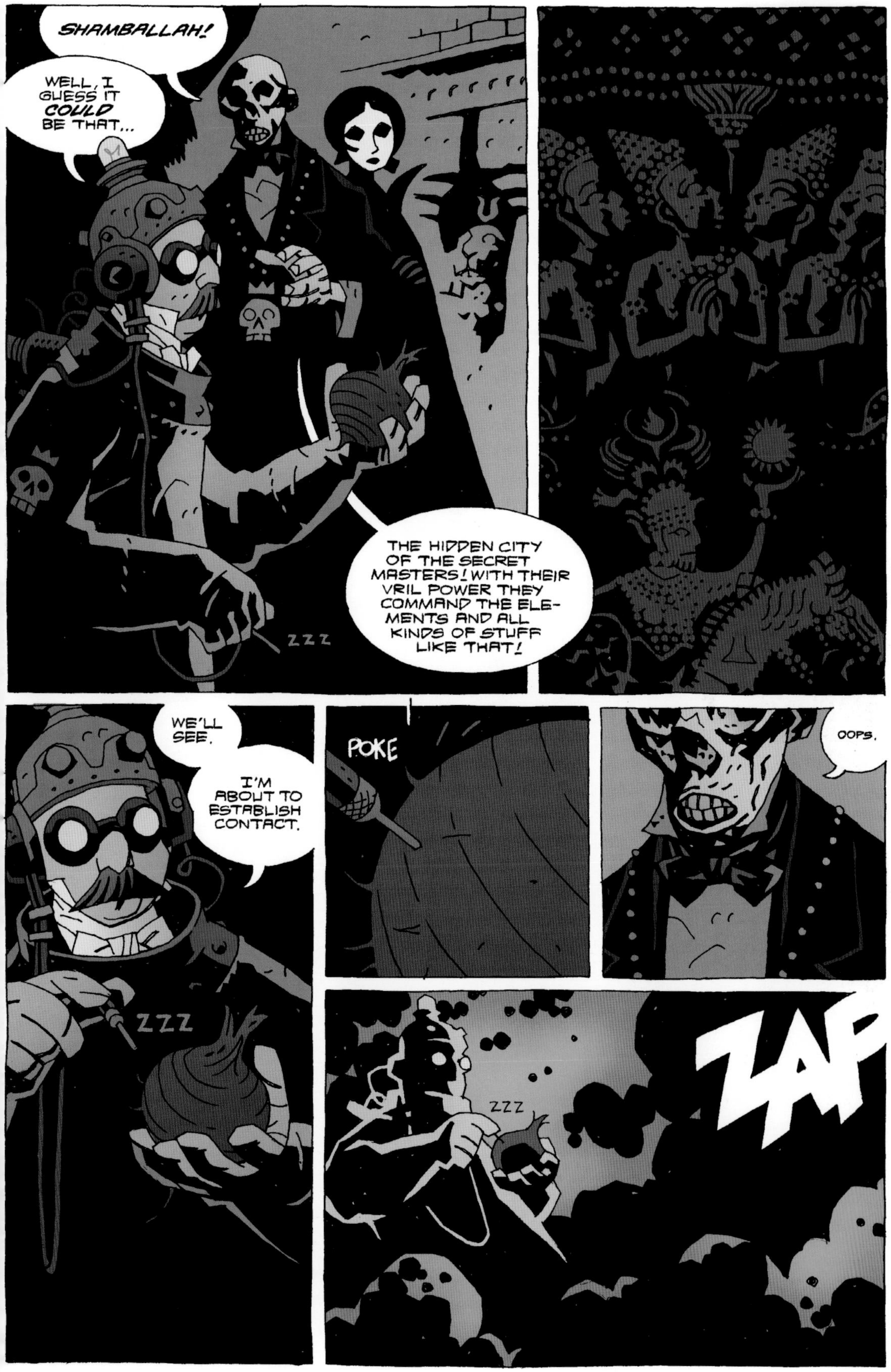
SHAMBALLAH!
WELL, I GUESS IT COULD BE THAT...
THE HIDDEN CITY OF THE SECRET MASTERS! WITH THEIR VRIL POWER THEY COMMAND THE ELE-MENTS AND ALL KINDS OF STUFF LIKE THAT!
ZZZ
WE'LL SEE.
I'M ABOUT TO ESTABLISH CONTACT.
ZZZ
POKE
OOPS.
ZZZ
ZAP

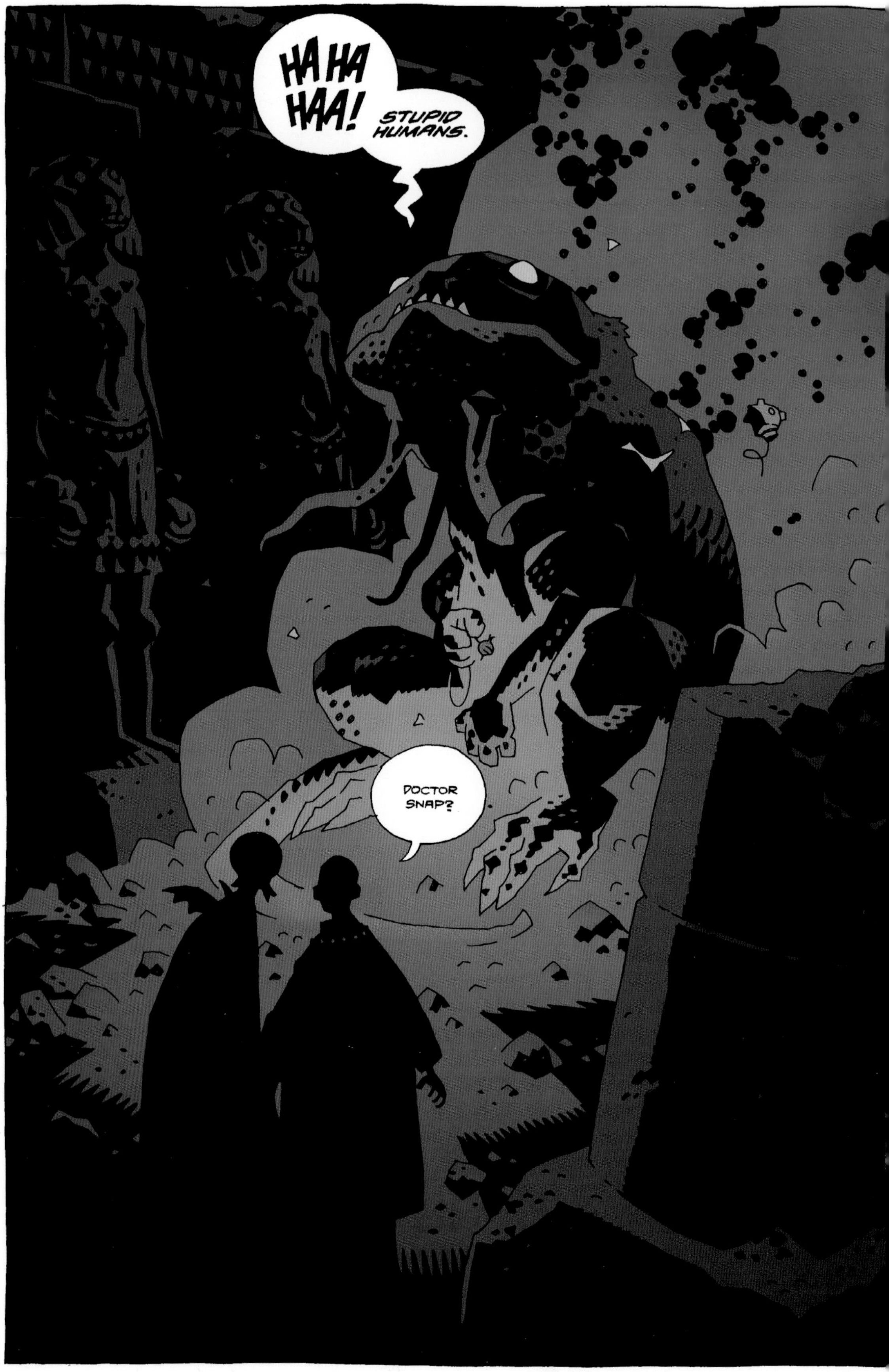
HA HA HAA!
STUPID HUMANS.
DOCTOR SNAP?

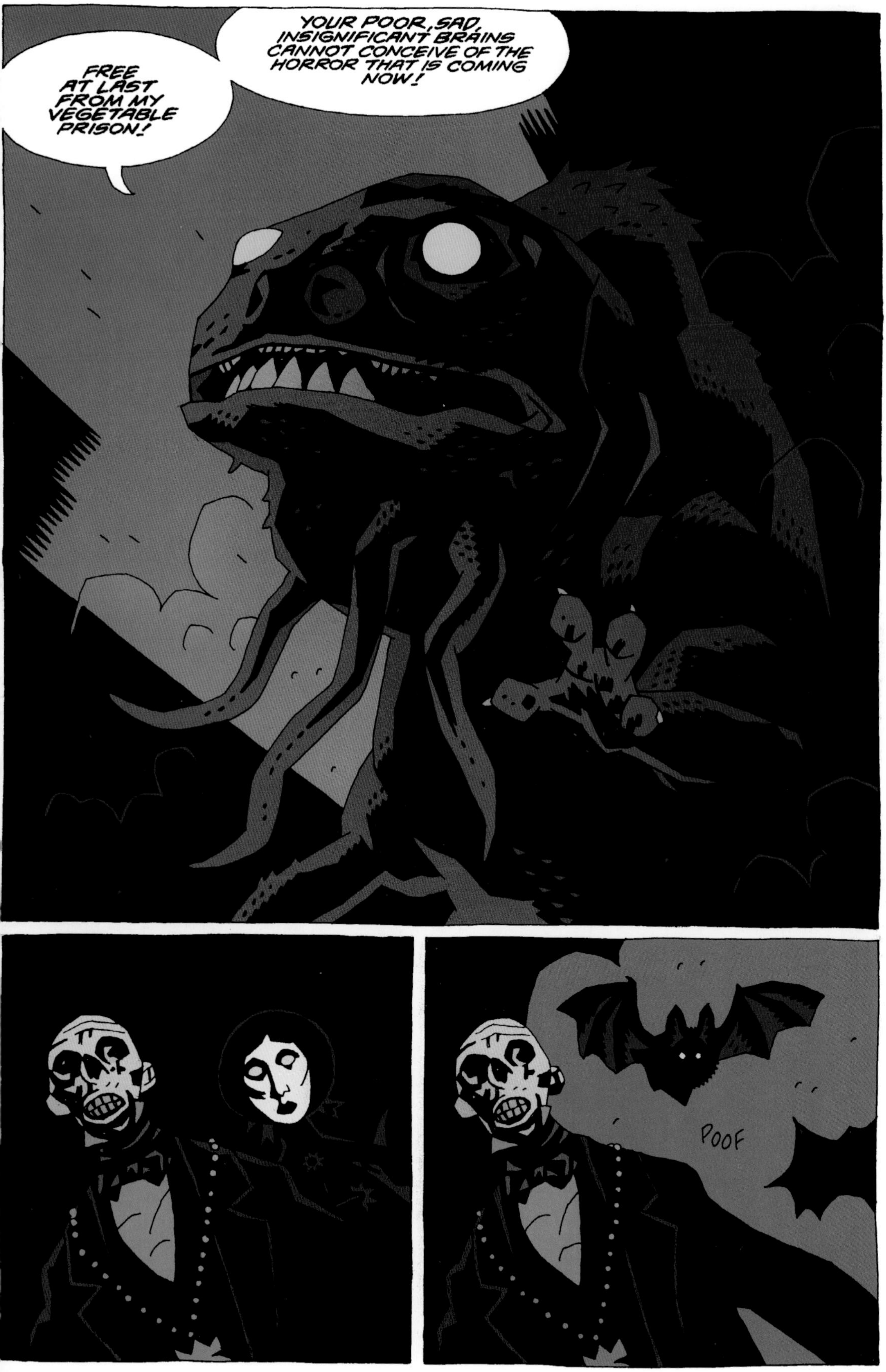
FREE AT LAST FROM MY VEGETABLE PRISON!
YOUR POOR, SAD, INSIGNIFICANT BRAINS CANNOT CONCEIVE OF THE HORROR THAT IS COMING NOW!
POOF

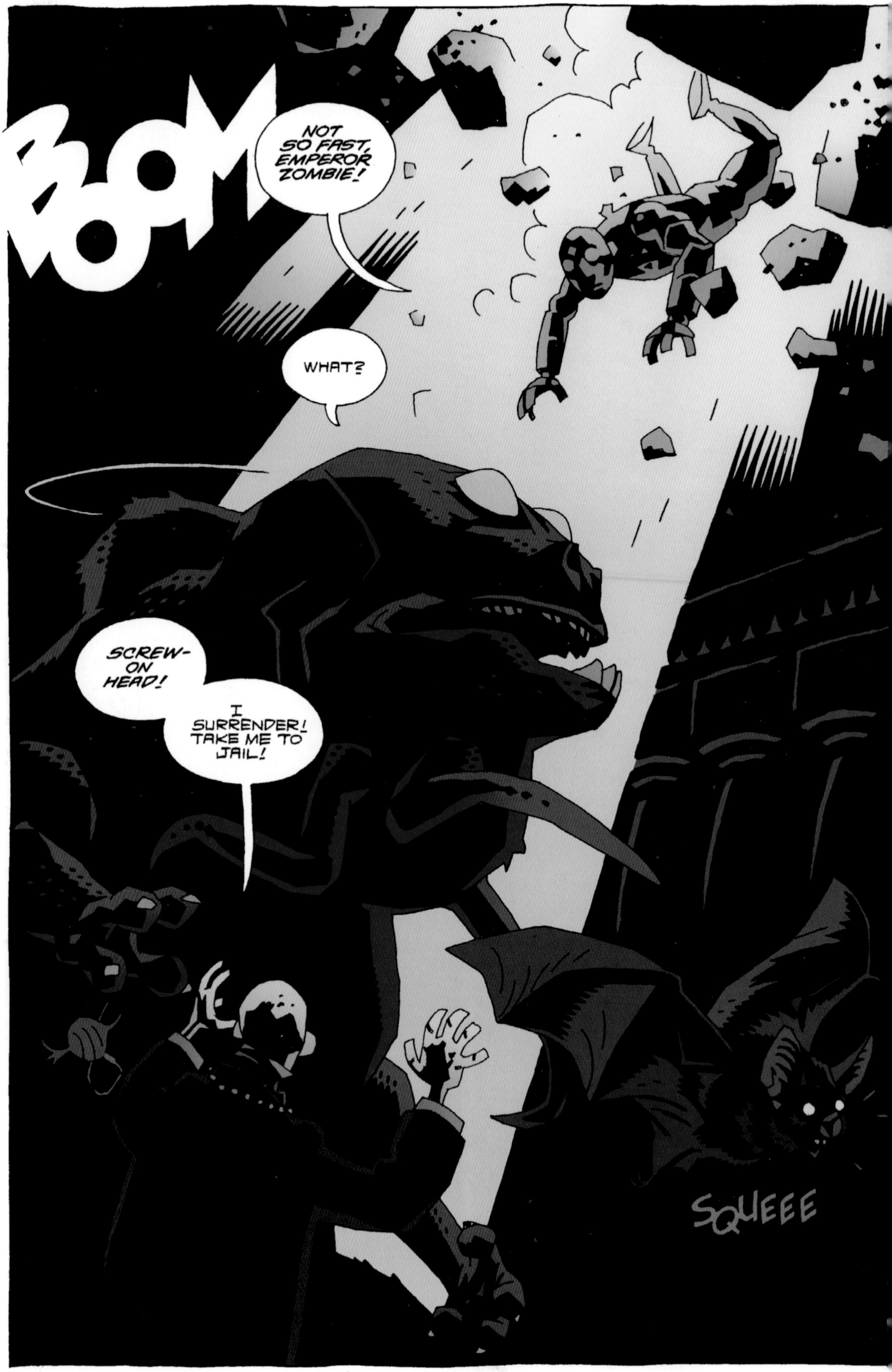
BOOM
NOT SO FAST, EMPEROR ZOMBIE!
WHAT?
SCREW-ON HEAD!
I SURRENDER! TAKE ME TO JAIL!
SQUEEE

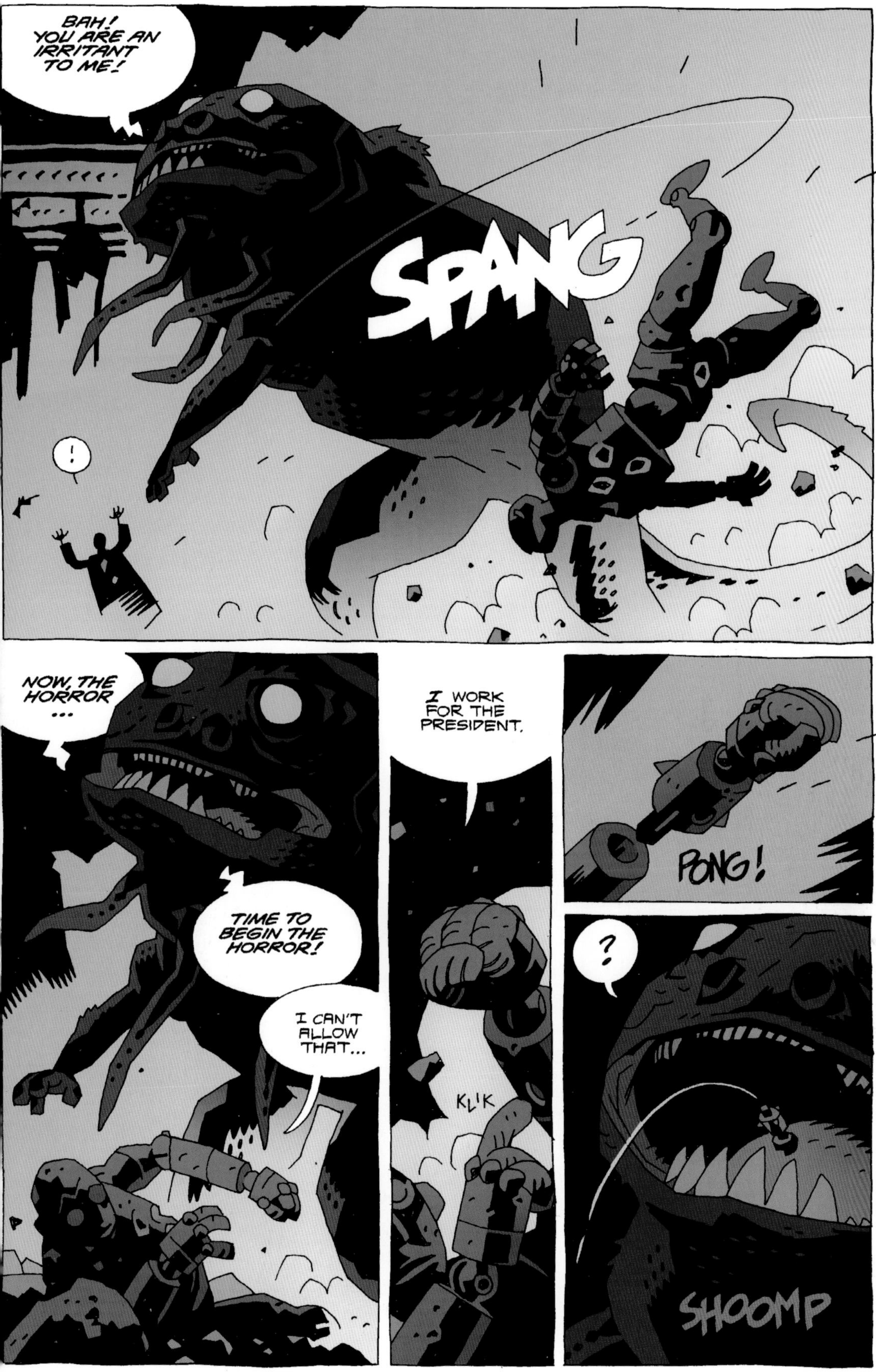
BAH! YOU ARE AN IRRITANT TO ME!
SPANG
!
NOW, THE HORROR ...
TIME TO BEGIN THE HORROR!
I CAN'T ALLOW THAT...
I WORK FOR THE PRESIDENT.
KLIK
PONG!
?
SHOOMP

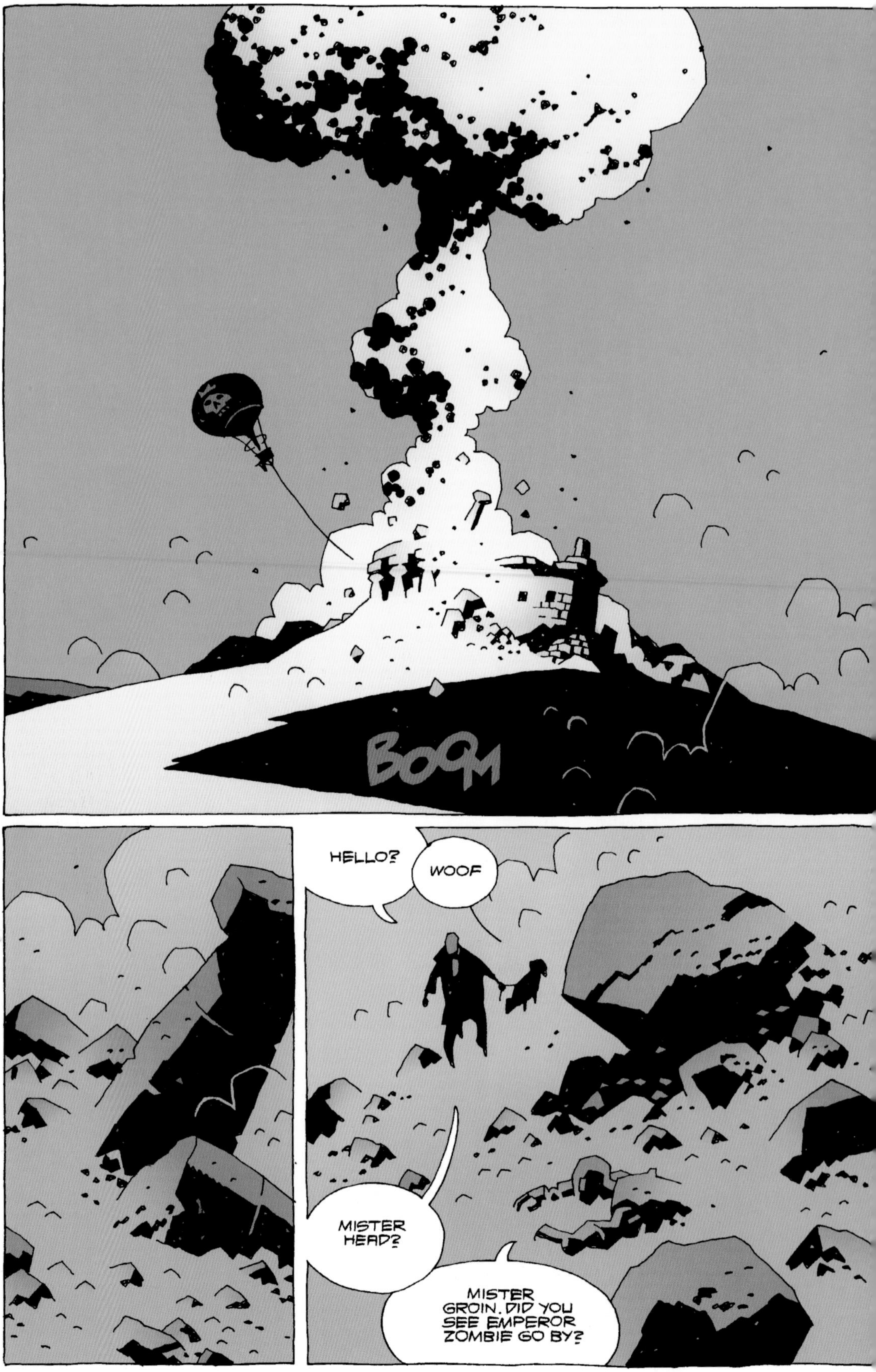
BOOM
HELLO?
WOOF
MISTER HEAD?
MISTER GROIN. DID YOU SEE EMPEROR ZOMBIE GO BY?

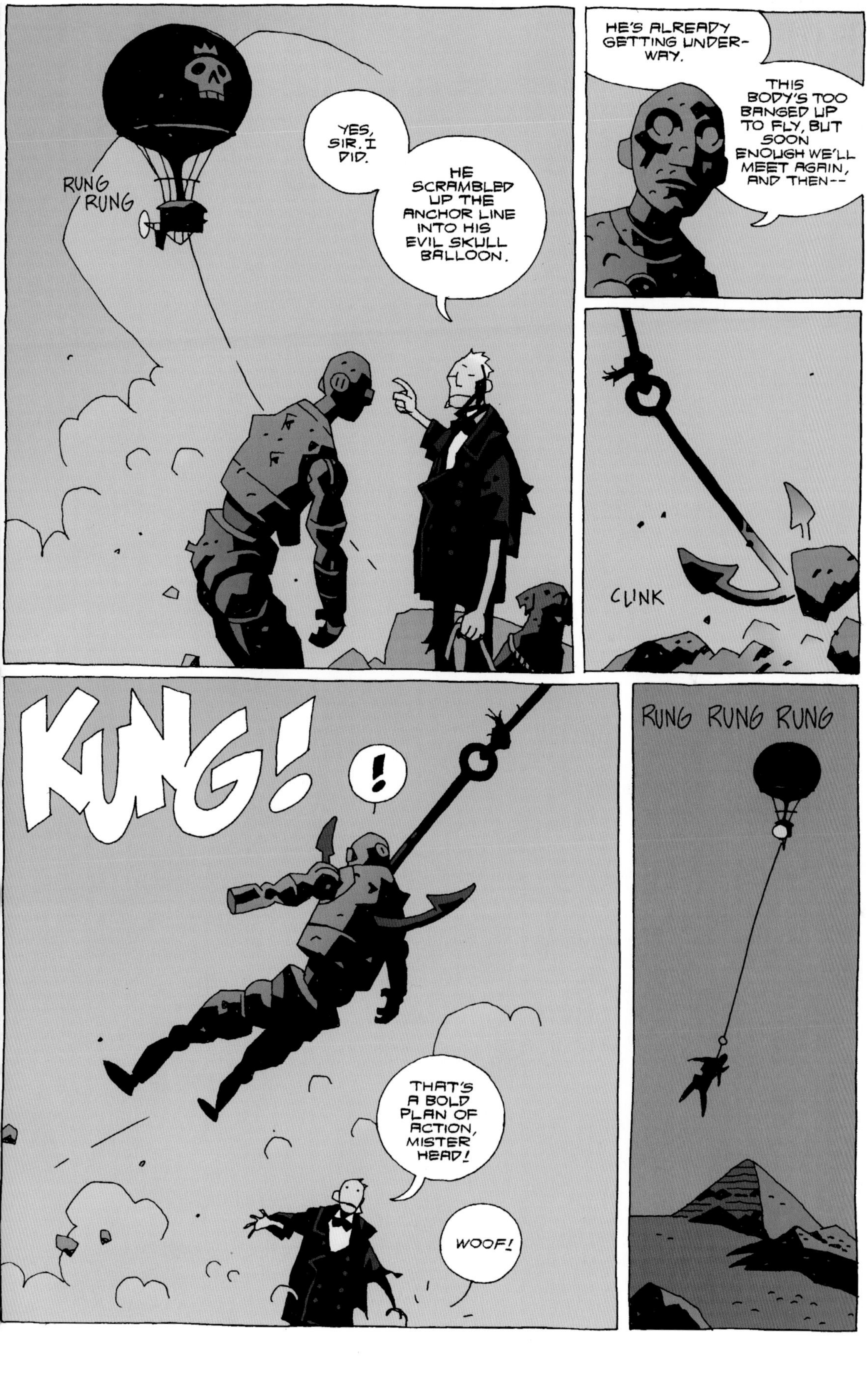
RUNG RUNG
YES, SIR. I DID.
HE SCRAMBLED UP THE ANCHOR LINE INTO HIS EVIL SKULL BALLOON.
HE'S ALREADY GETTING UNDER-WAY.
THIS BODY'S TOO BANGED UP TO FLY, BUT SOON ENOUGH WE'LL MEET AGAIN, AND THEN--
CLINK
KUNG!
!
THAT'S A BOLD PLAN OF ACTION, MISTER HEAD!
WOOF!
RUNG RUNG RUNG

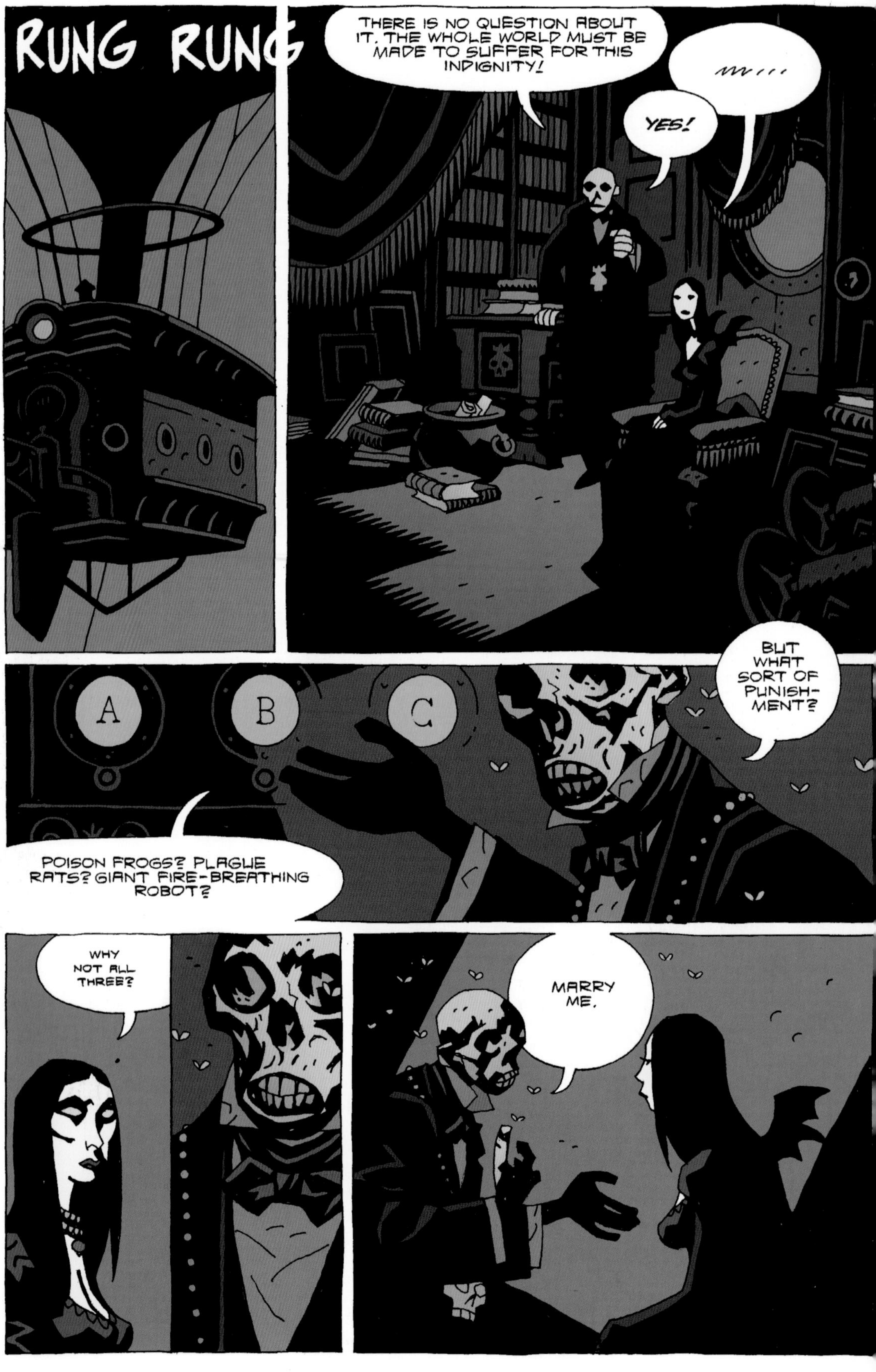
RUNG RUNG
THERE IS NO QUESTION ABOUT IT. THE WHOLE WORLD MUST BE MADE TO SUFFER FOR THIS INDIGNITY!
YES!
BUT WHAT SORT OF PUNISH-MENT?
A
B
C
POISON FROGS? PLAGUE RATS? GIANT FIRE-BREATHING ROBOT?
WHY NOT ALL THREE?
MARRY ME.

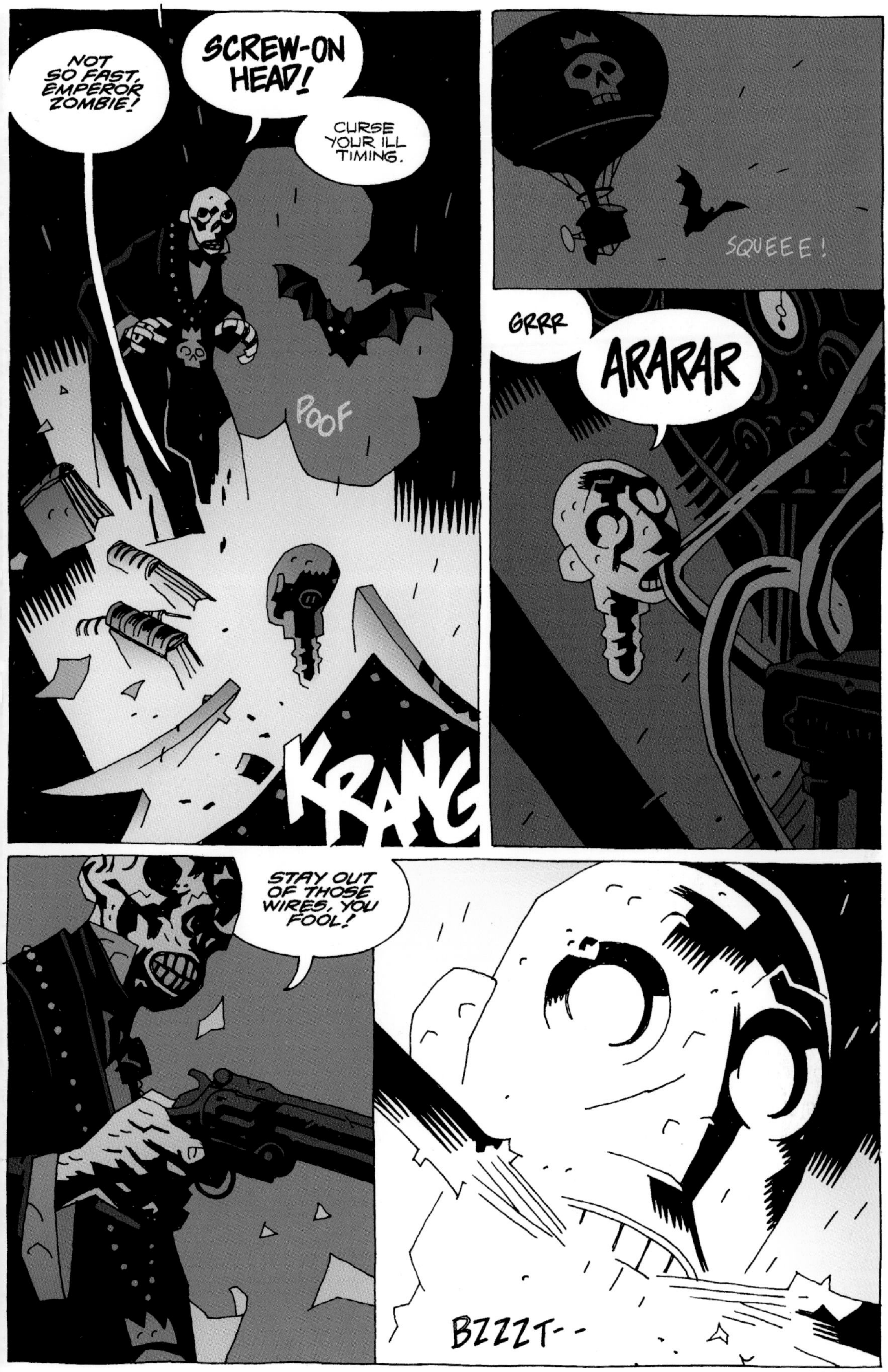

NOT SO FAST, EMPEROR ZOMBIE!
SCREW-ON HEAD!
CURSE YOUR ILL TIMING.
POOF
KRANG
SQUEEE!
GRRR
ARARAR
STAY OUT OF THOSE WIRES, YOU FOOL!
BZZZT--

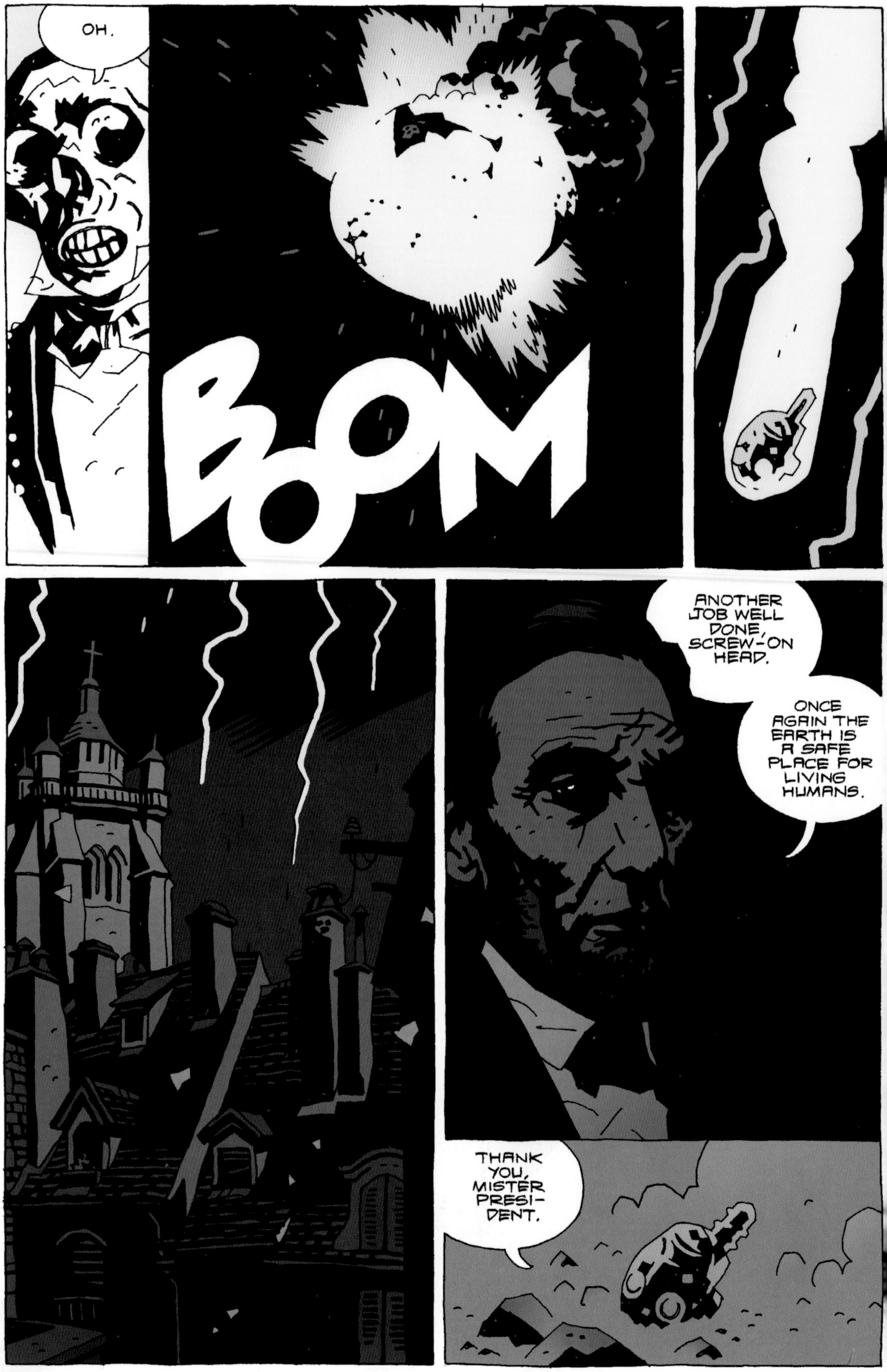
OH.
BOOM
ANOTHER JOB WELL DONE, SCREW-ON HEAD.
ONCE AGAIN THE EARTH IS A SAFE PLACE FOR LIVING HUMANS.
THANK YOU, MISTER PRESI-DENT.

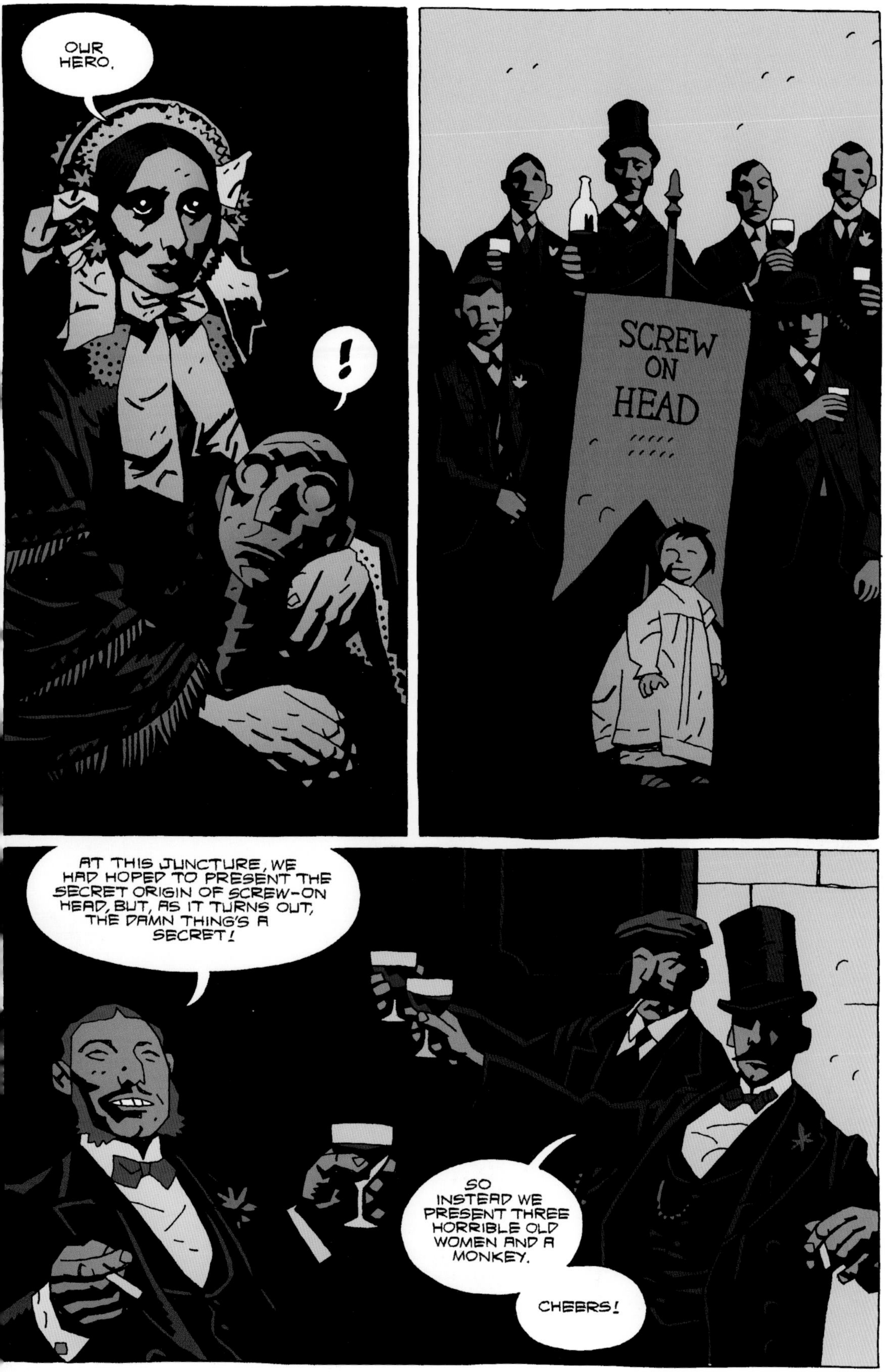
OUR HERO.
!
SCREW ON HEAD
AT THIS JUNCTURE, WE HAD HOPED TO PRESENT THE SECRET ORIGIN OF SCREW-ON HEAD, BUT, AS IT TURNS OUT, THE DAMN THING'S A SECRET!
SO INSTEAD WE PRESENT THREE HORRIBLE OLD WOMEN AND A MONKEY.
CHEERS!

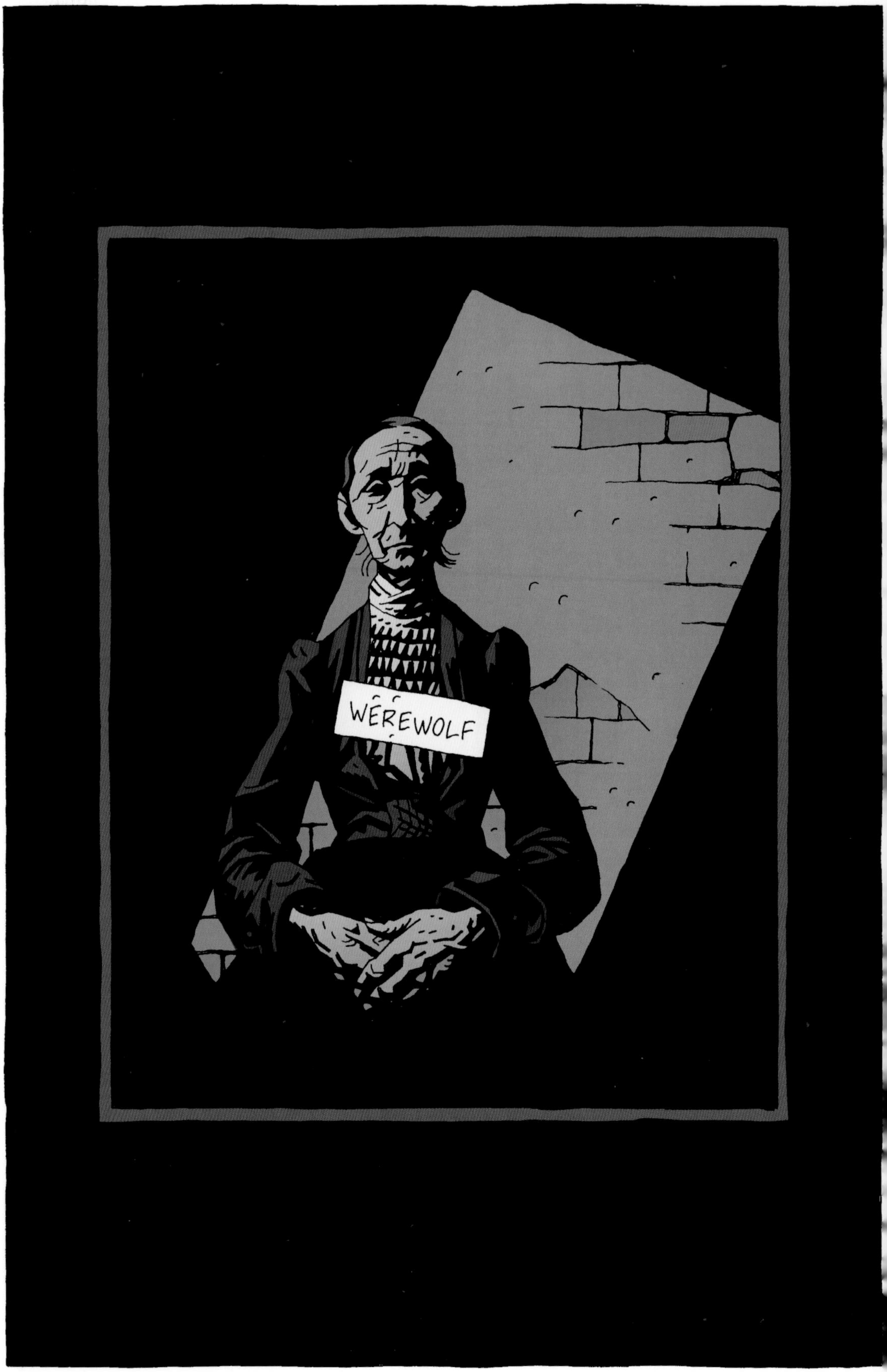
WEREWOLF

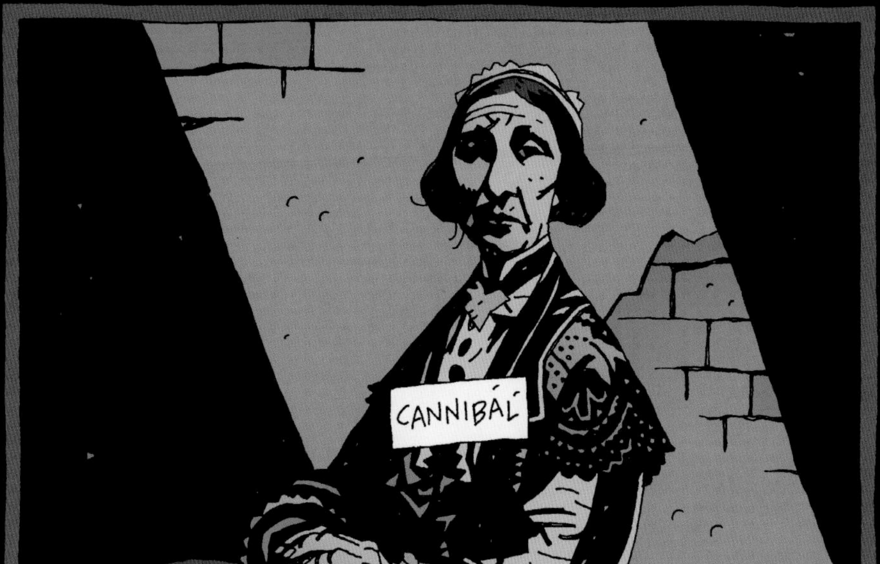
CANNIBAL

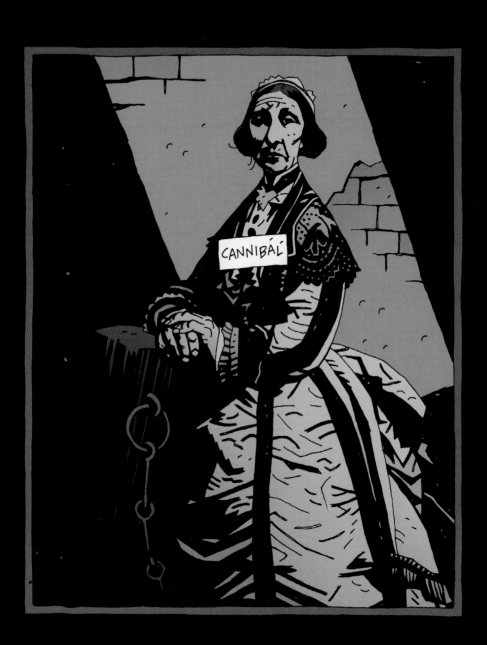

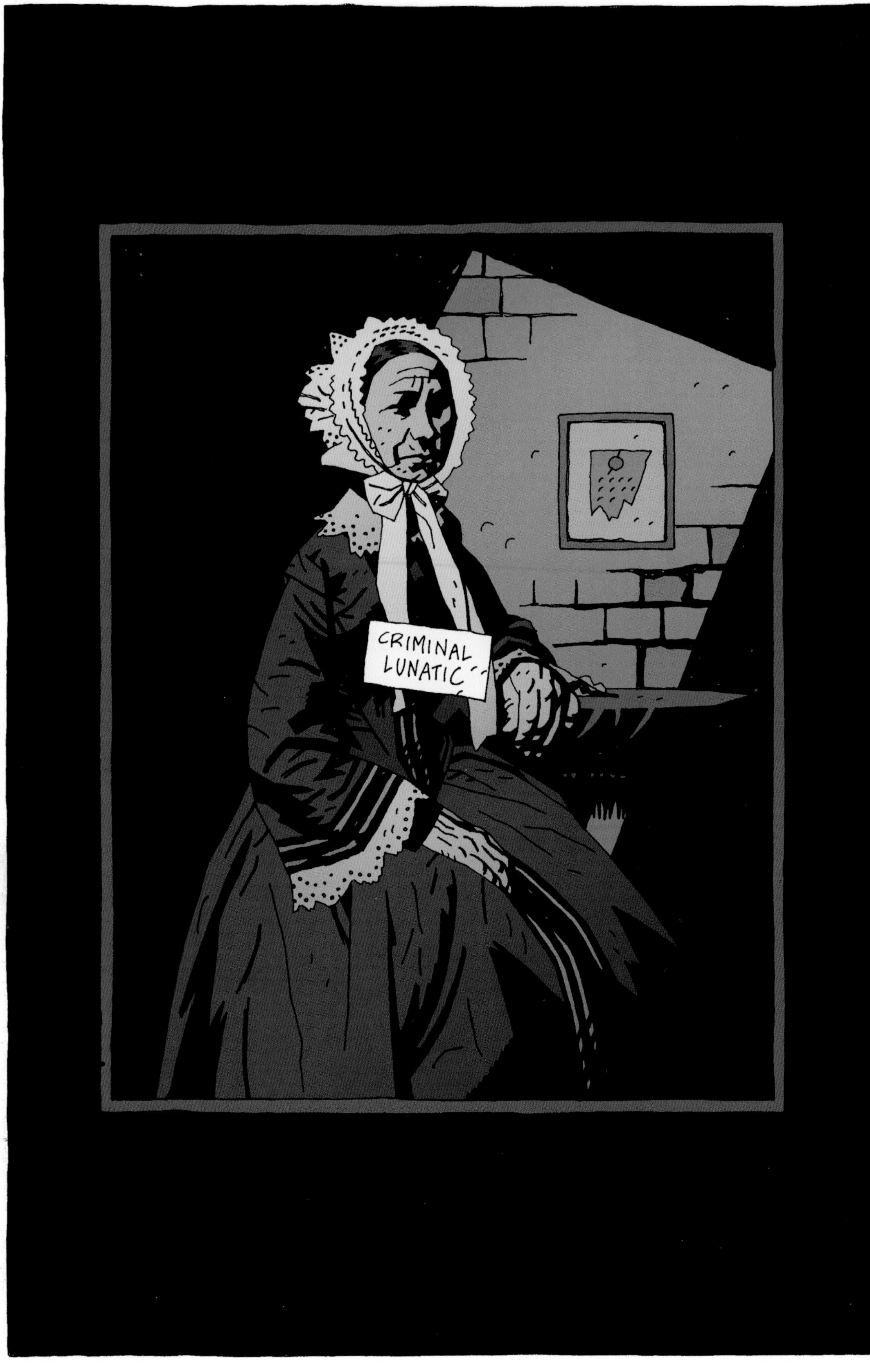
CRIMINAL LUNATIC

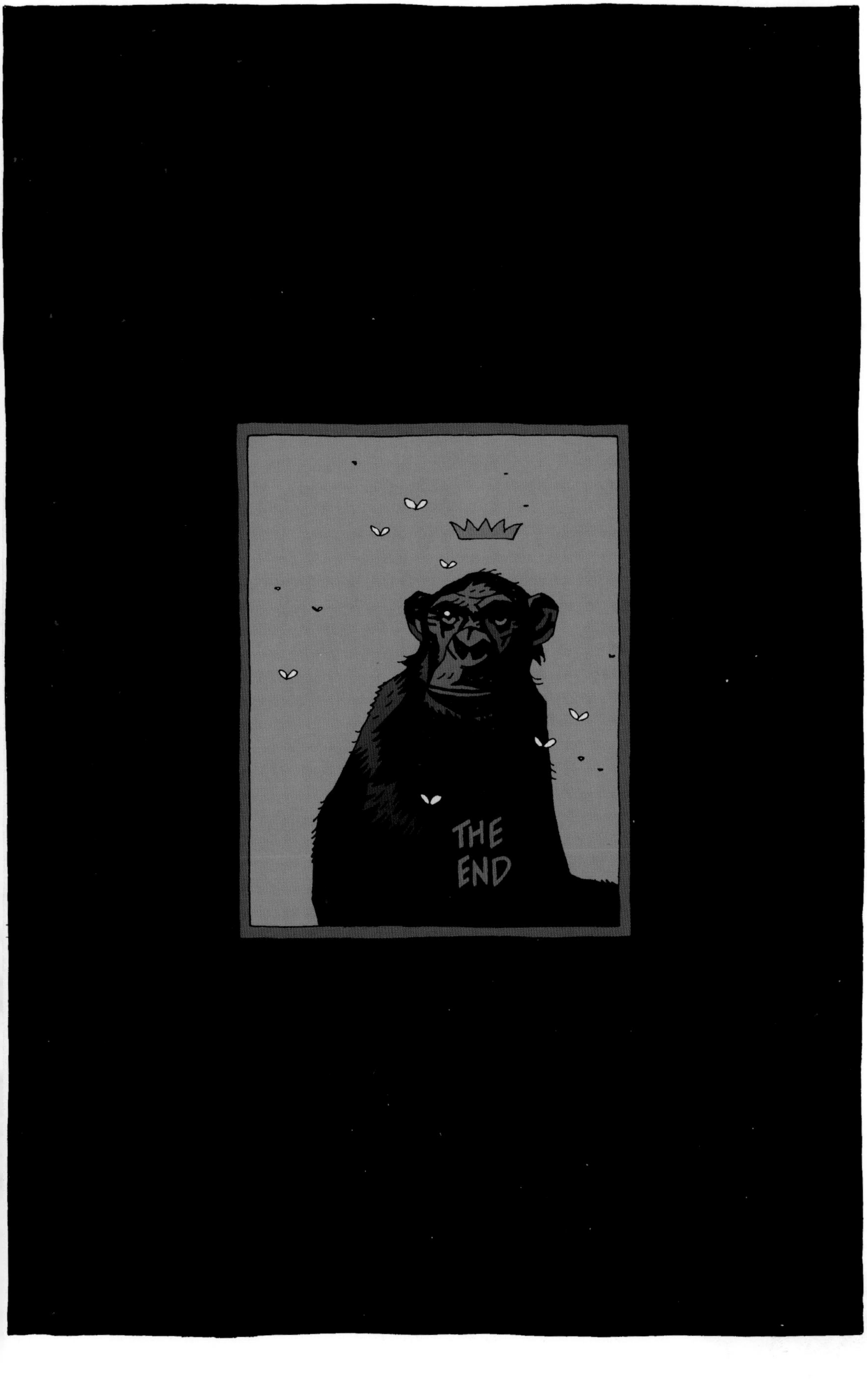
THE END

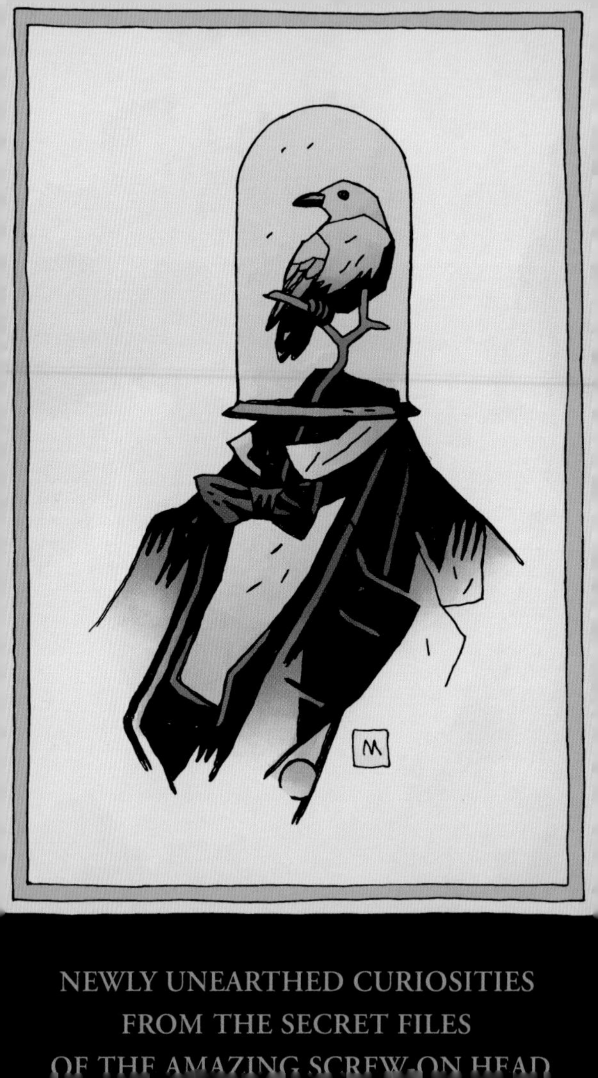

NEWLY UNEARTHED CURIOSITIES
FROM THE SECRET FILES
OF THE AMAZING SCREW-ON HEAD

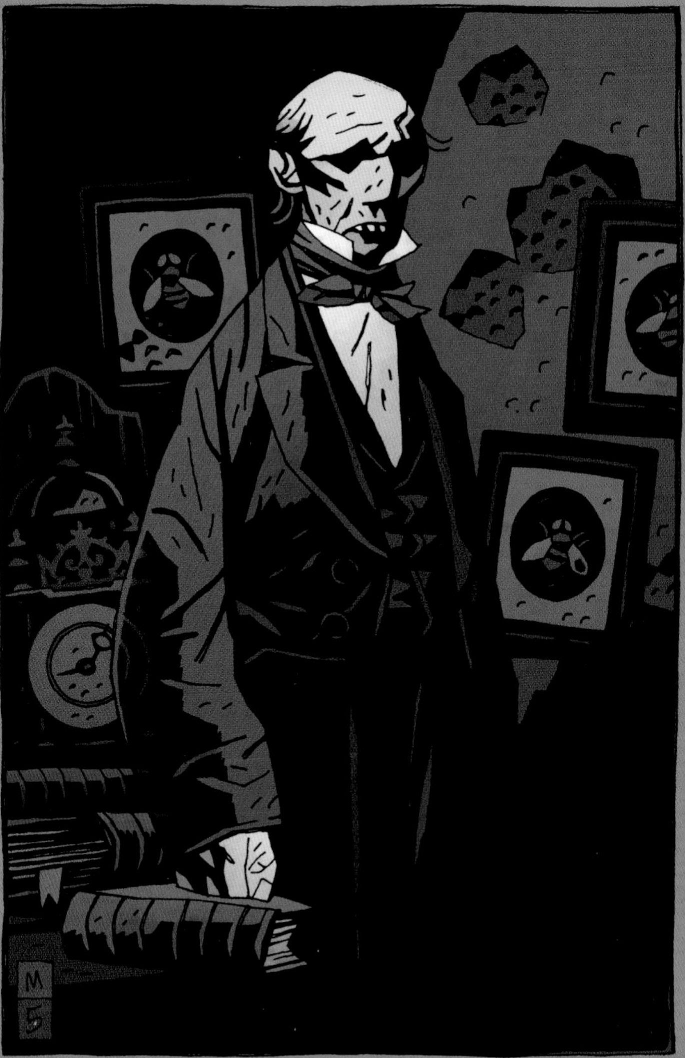

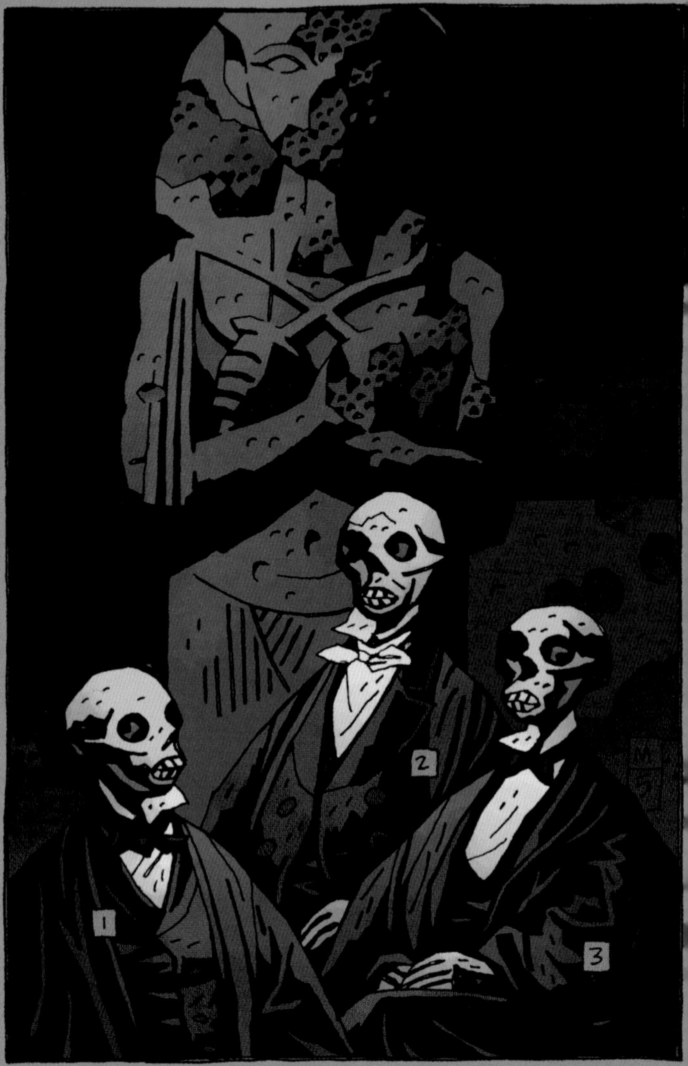
1
2
3

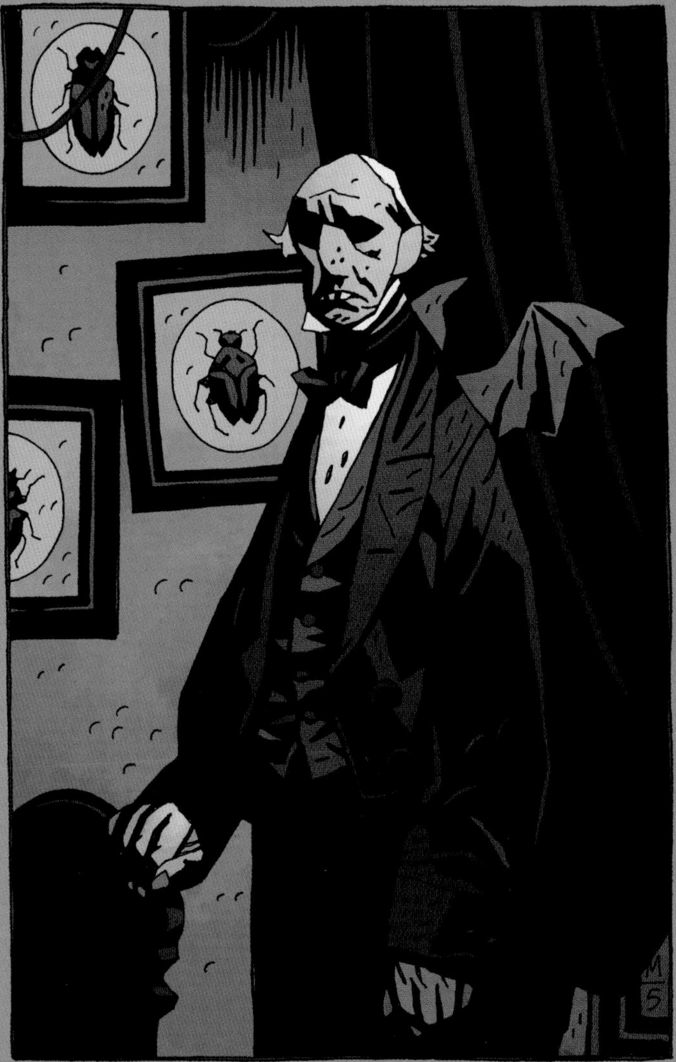

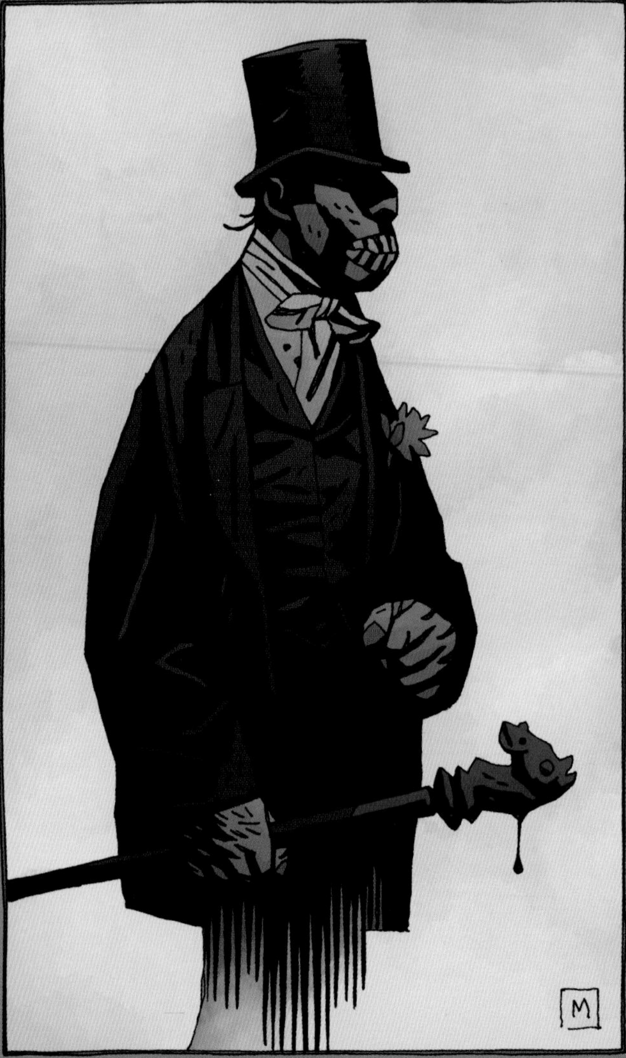

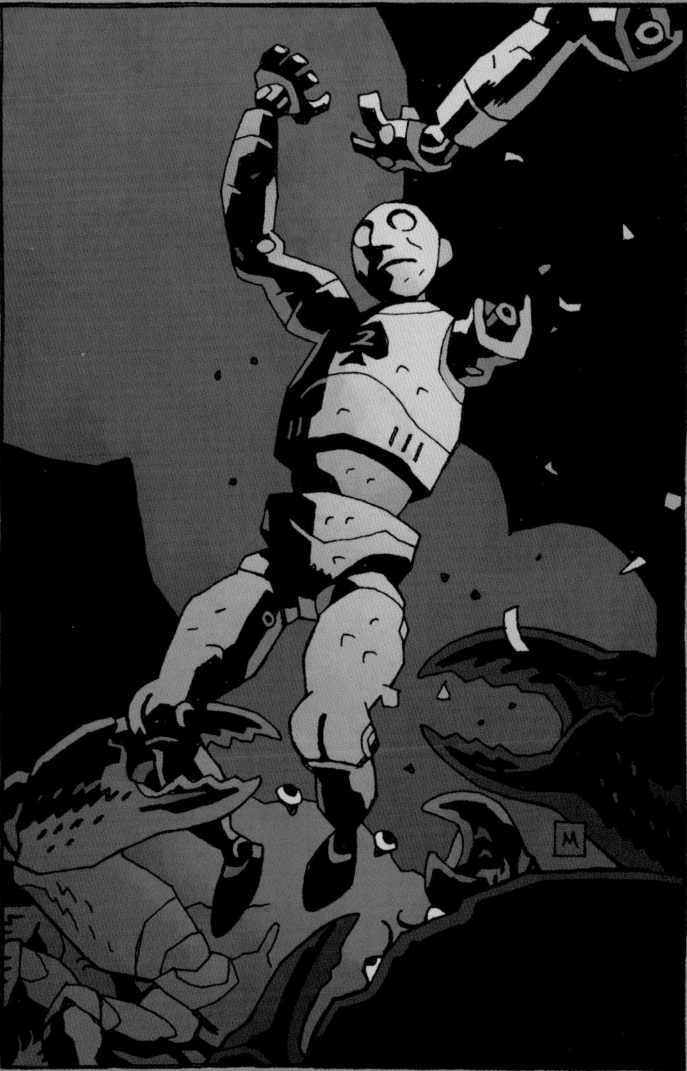

PART TWO

OTHER CURIOUS OBJECTS

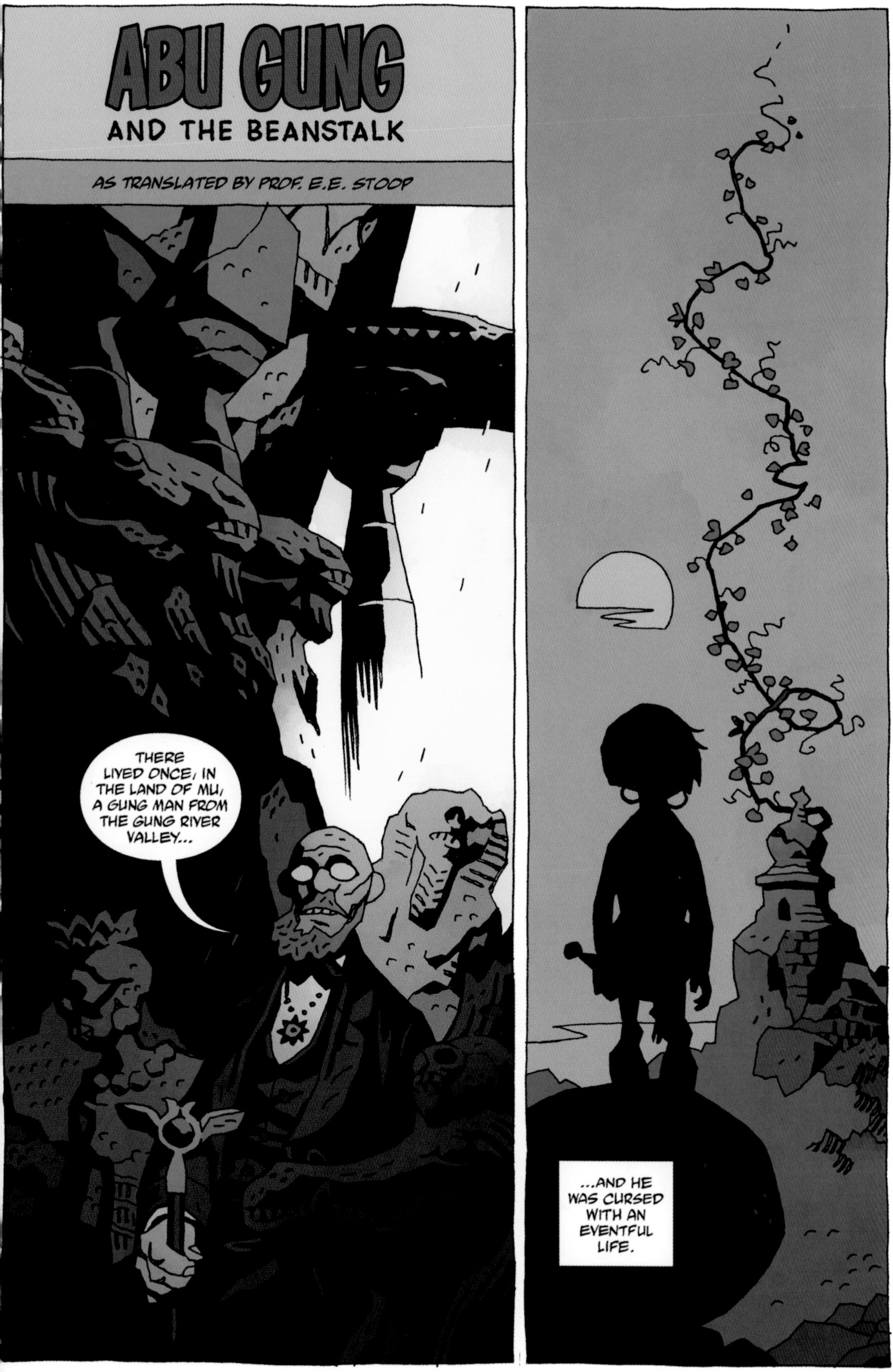

ABU GUNG
AND THE BEANSTALK
AS TRANSLATED BY PROF. E.E. STOOP
THERE LIVED ONCE, IN THE LAND OF MU, A GUNG MAN FROM THE GUNG RIVER VALLEY...
...AND HE WAS CURSED WITH AN EVENTFUL LIFE.

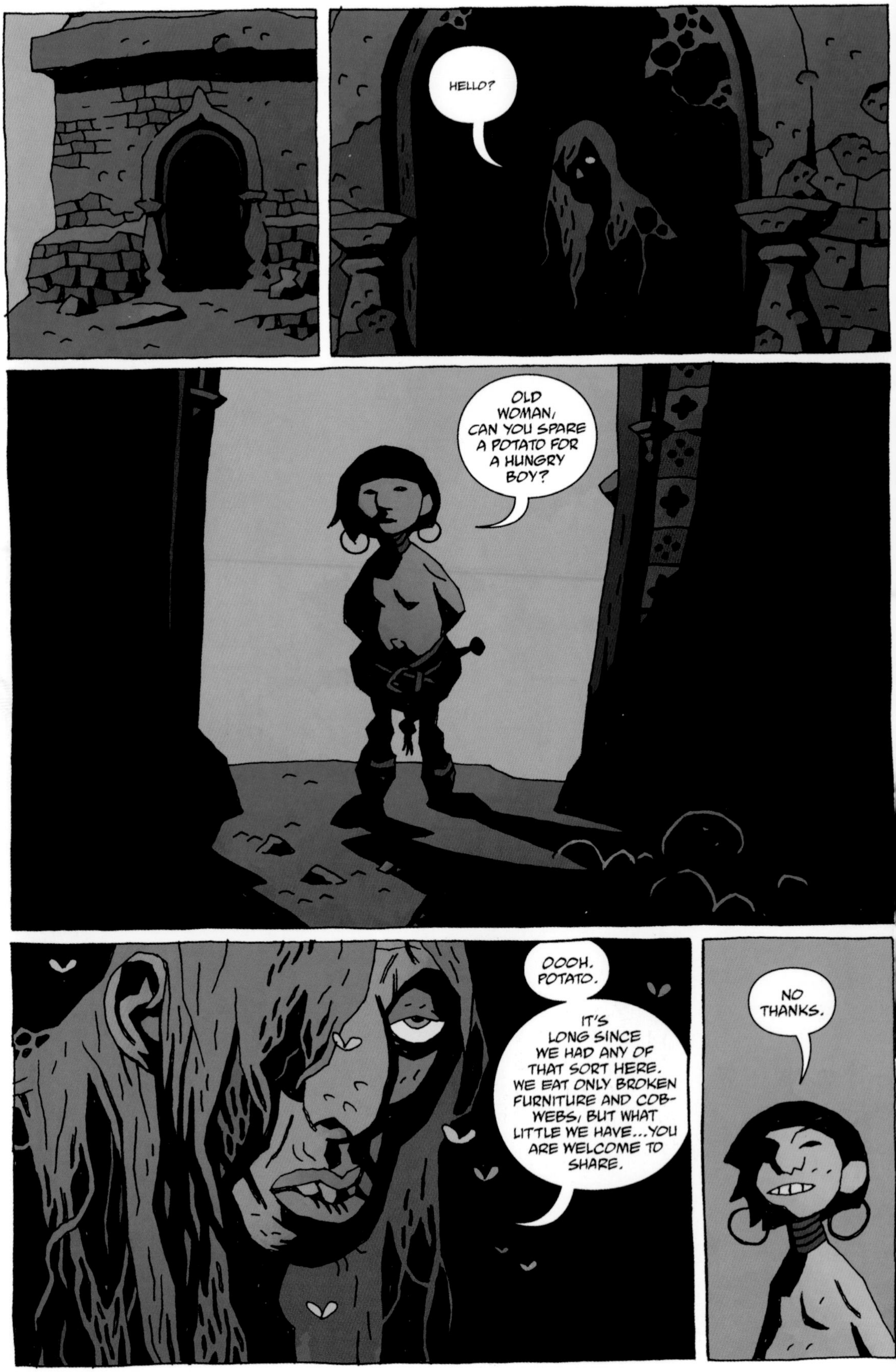
HELLO?
OLD WOMAN, CAN YOU SPARE A POTATO FOR A HUNGRY BOY?
OOOH. POTATO.
IT'S LONG SINCE WE HAD ANY OF THAT SORT HERE. WE EAT ONLY BROKEN FURNITURE AND COB-WEBS, BUT WHAT LITTLE WE HAVE...YOU ARE WELCOME TO SHARE.
NO THANKS.

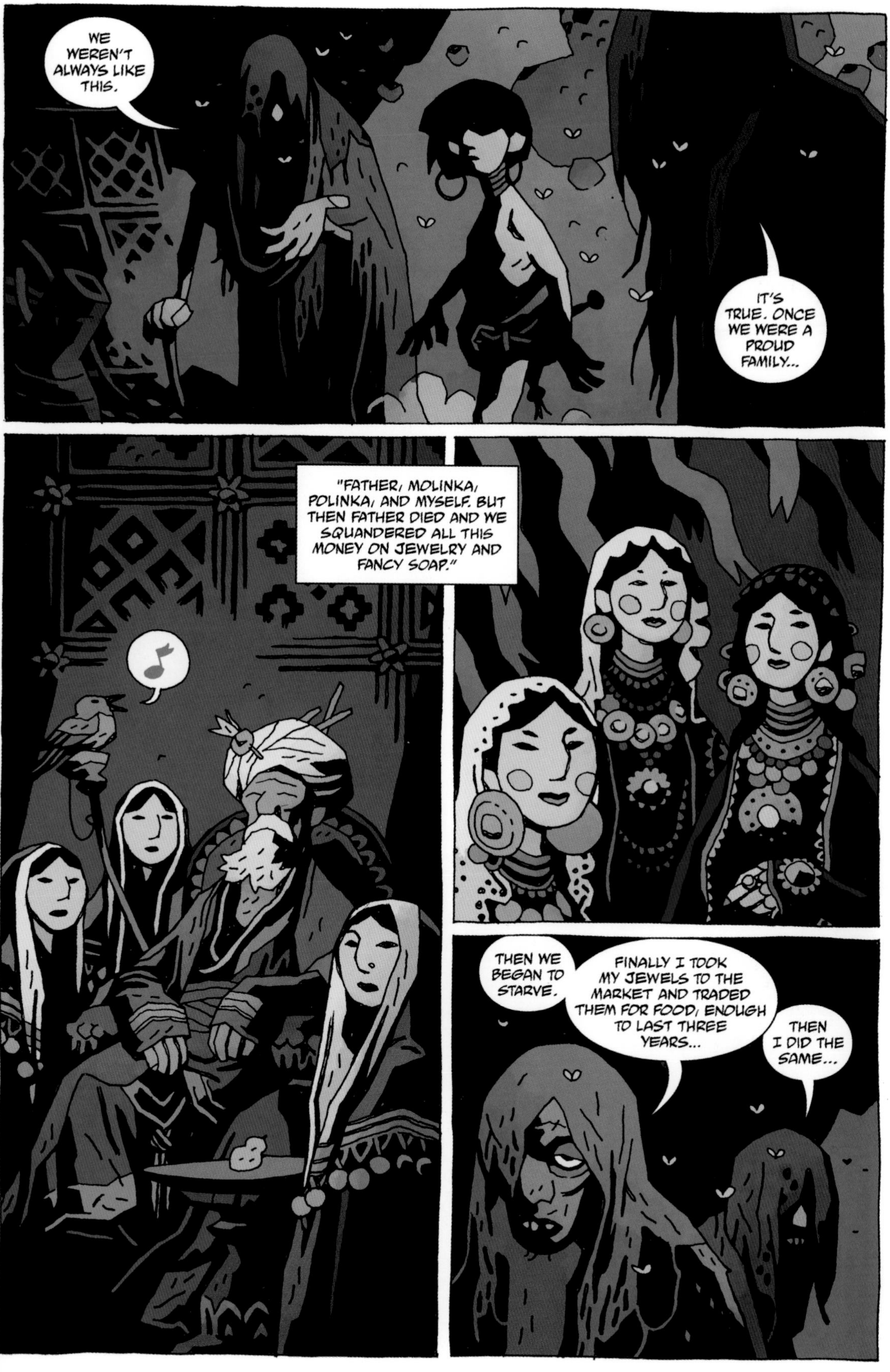
WE WEREN'T ALWAYS LIKE THIS.
IT'S TRUE. ONCE WE WERE A PROUD FAMILY...
"FATHER, MOLINKA, POLINKA, AND MYSELF. BUT THEN FATHER DIED AND WE SQUANDERED ALL THIS MONEY ON JEWELRY AND FANCY SOAP."
THEN WE BEGAN TO STARVE.
FINALLY I TOOK MY JEWELS TO THE MARKET AND TRADED THEM FOR FOOD, ENOUGH TO LAST THREE YEARS...
THEN I DID THE SAME...

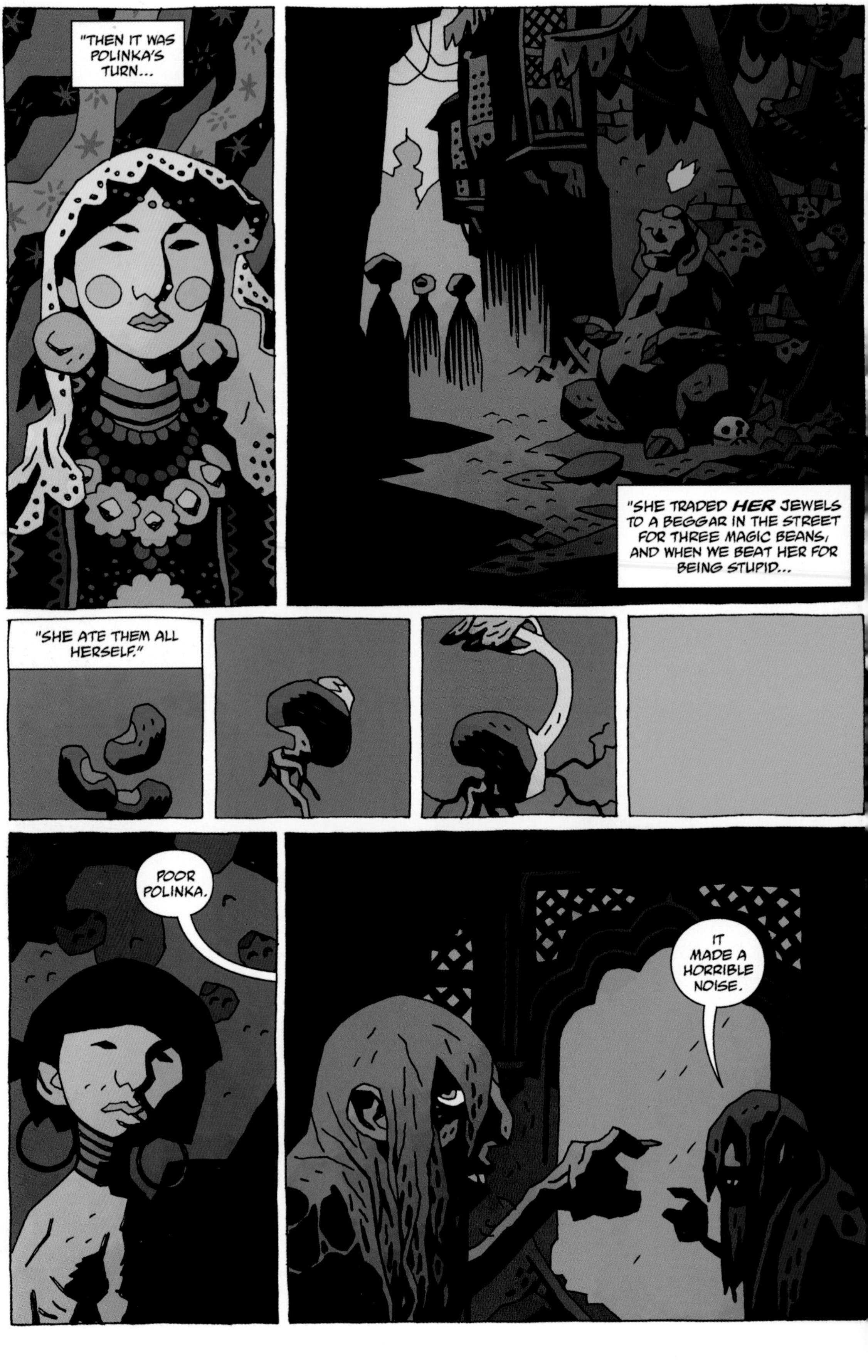
"THEN IT WAS POLINKA'S TURN...
"SHE TRADED **HER** JEWELS TO A BEGGAR IN THE STREET FOR THREE MAGIC BEANS, AND WHEN WE BEAT HER FOR BEING STUPID...
"SHE ATE THEM ALL HERSELF."
POOR POLINKA.
IT MADE A HORRIBLE NOISE.

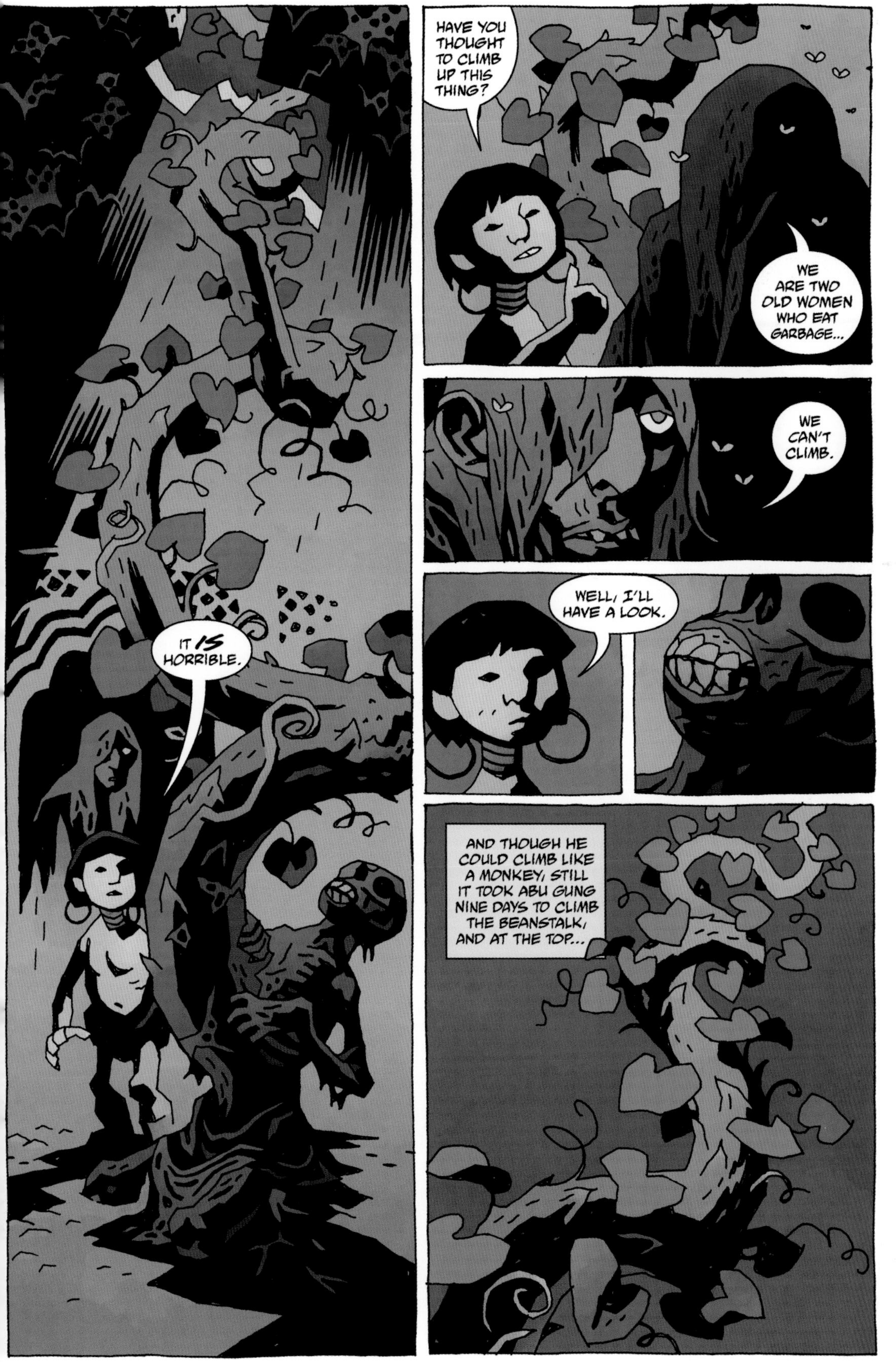
IT IS HORRIBLE.
HAVE YOU THOUGHT TO CLIMB UP THIS THING?
WE ARE TWO OLD WOMEN WHO EAT GARBAGE...
WE CAN'T CLIMB.
WELL, I'LL HAVE A LOOK.
AND THOUGH HE COULD CLIMB LIKE A MONKEY, STILL IT TOOK ABU GUNG NINE DAYS TO CLIMB THE BEANSTALK, AND AT THE TOP...

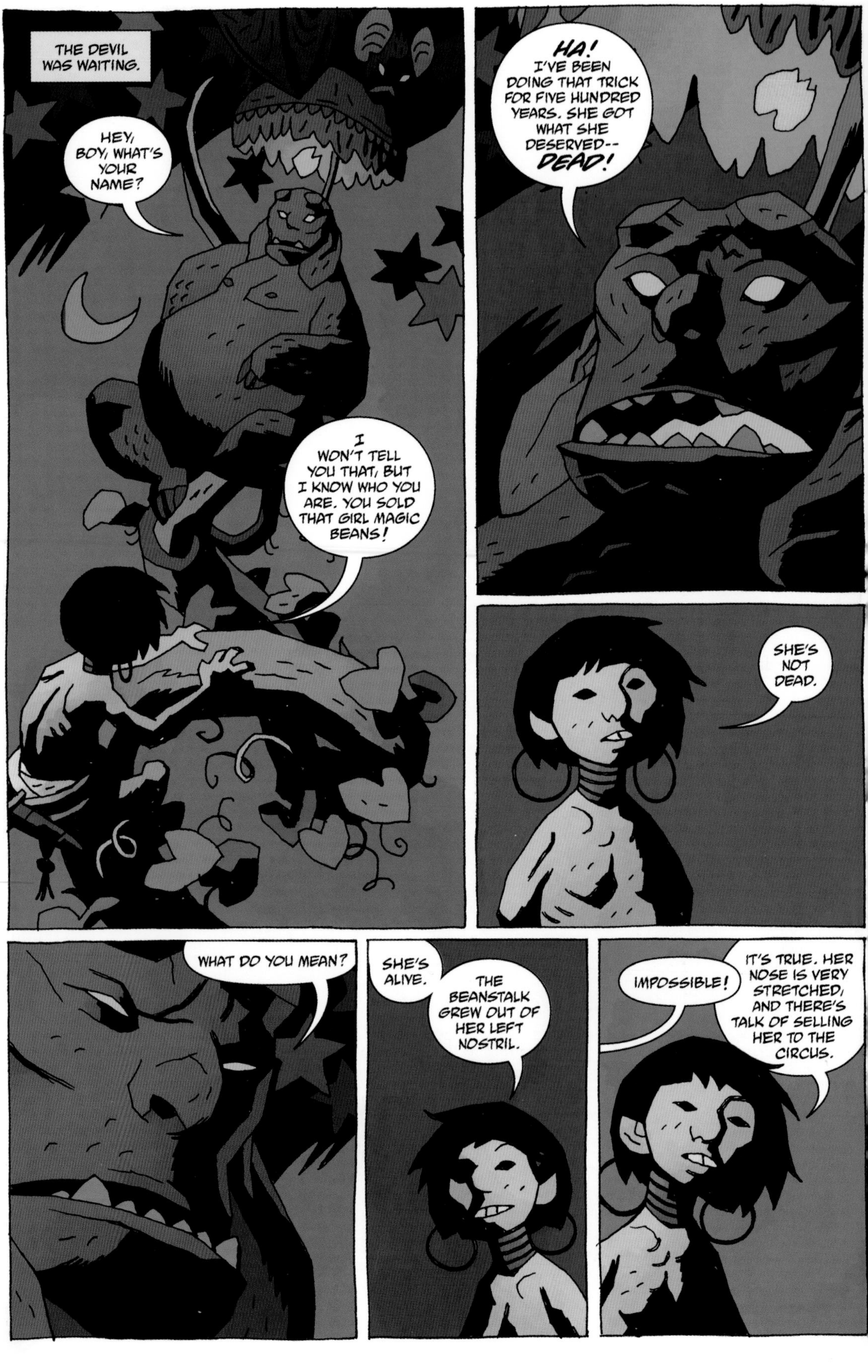

THE DEVIL WAS WAITING.
HEY, BOY, WHAT'S YOUR NAME?
I WON'T TELL YOU THAT, BUT I KNOW WHO YOU ARE. YOU SOLD THAT GIRL MAGIC BEANS!
HA! I'VE BEEN DOING THAT TRICK FOR FIVE HUNDRED YEARS. SHE GOT WHAT SHE DESERVED-- DEAD!
SHE'S NOT DEAD.
WHAT DO YOU MEAN?
SHE'S ALIVE.
THE BEANSTALK GREW OUT OF HER LEFT NOSTRIL.
IMPOSSIBLE!
IT'S TRUE. HER NOSE IS VERY STRETCHED, AND THERE'S TALK OF SELLING HER TO THE CIRCUS.

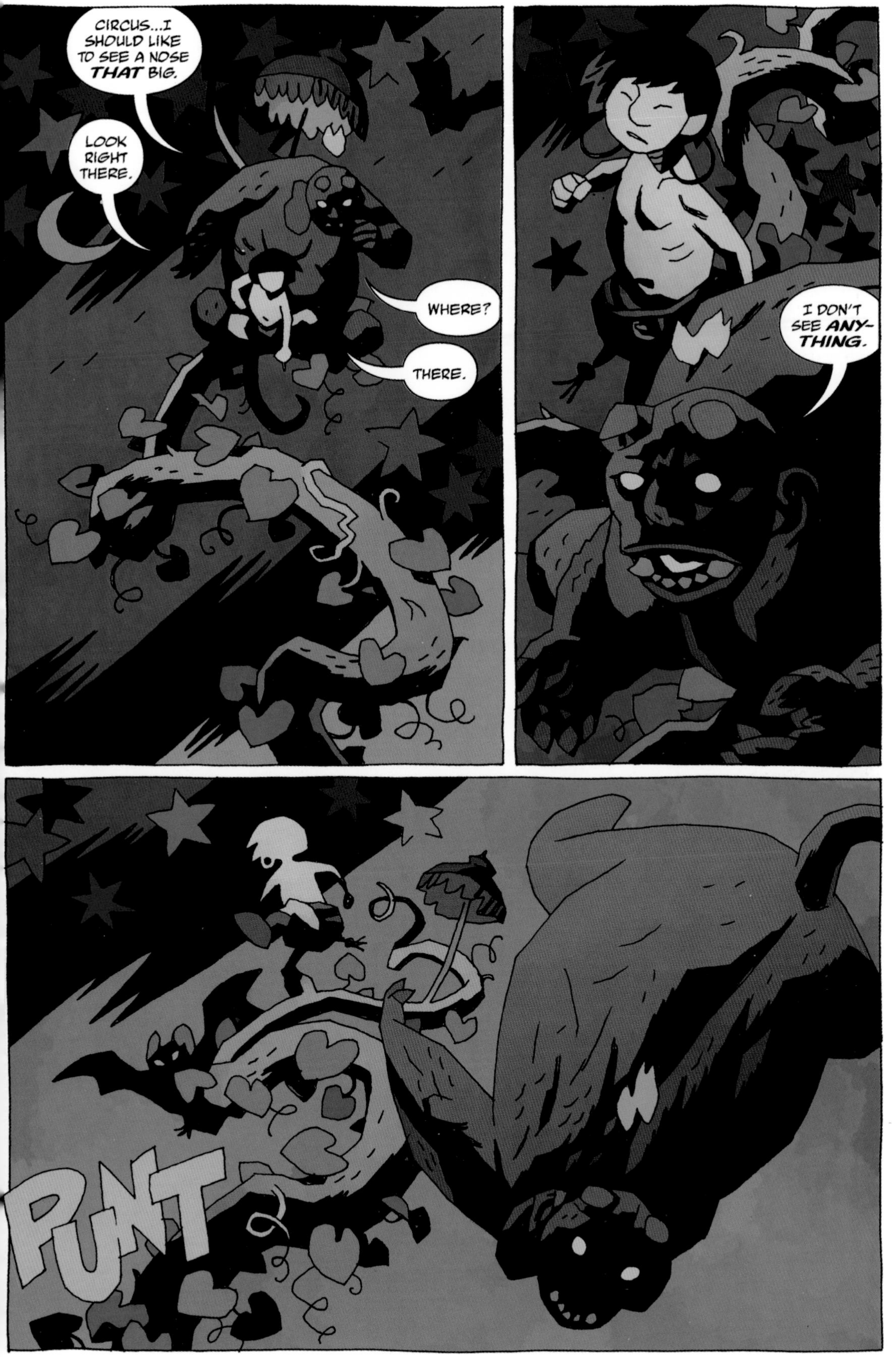
CIRCUS...I SHOULD LIKE TO SEE A NOSE THAT BIG.
LOOK RIGHT THERE.
WHERE?
THERE.
I DON'T SEE ANY-THING.
PUNT

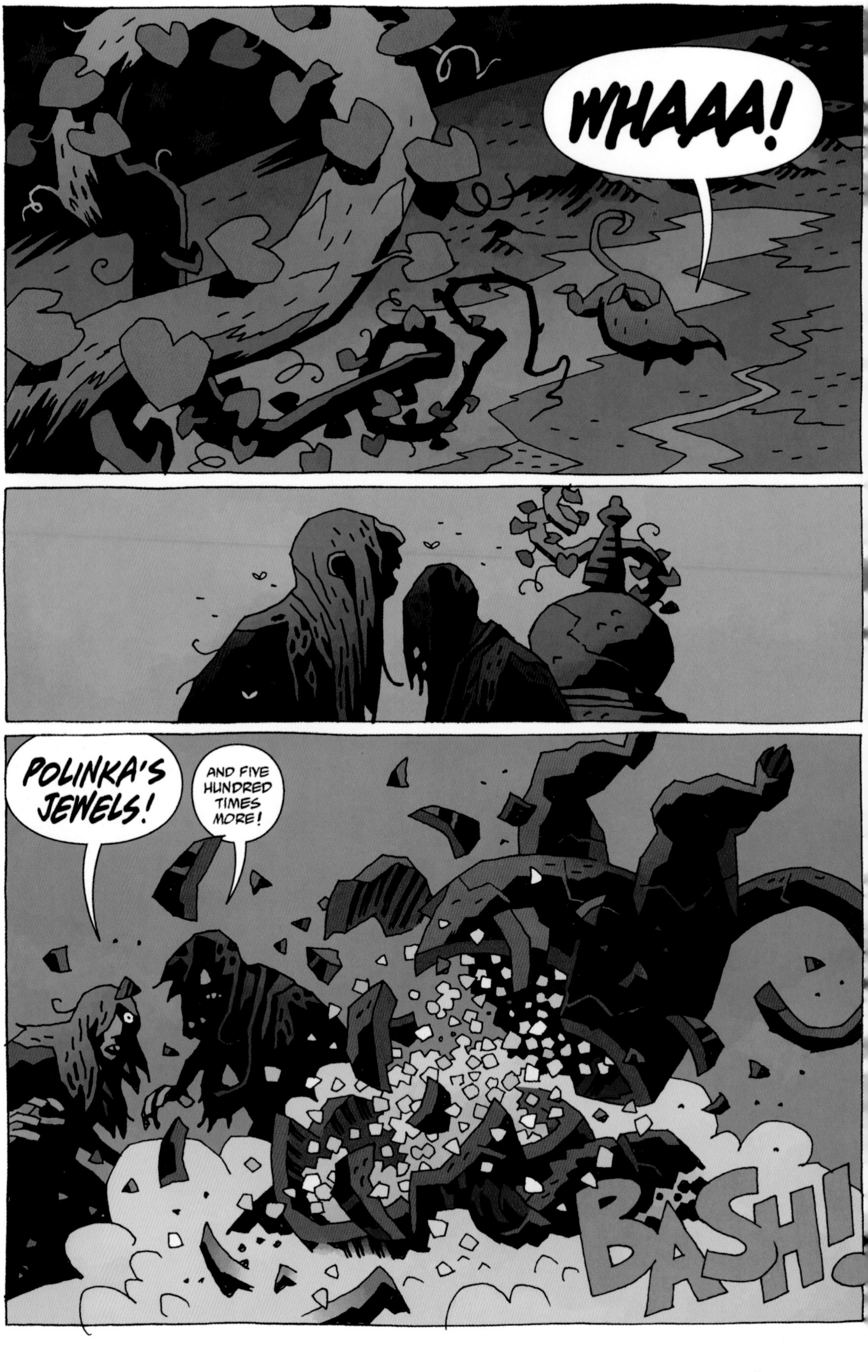
WHAAAA!
POLINKA'S JEWELS!
AND FIVE HUNDRED TIMES MORE!
BASH!

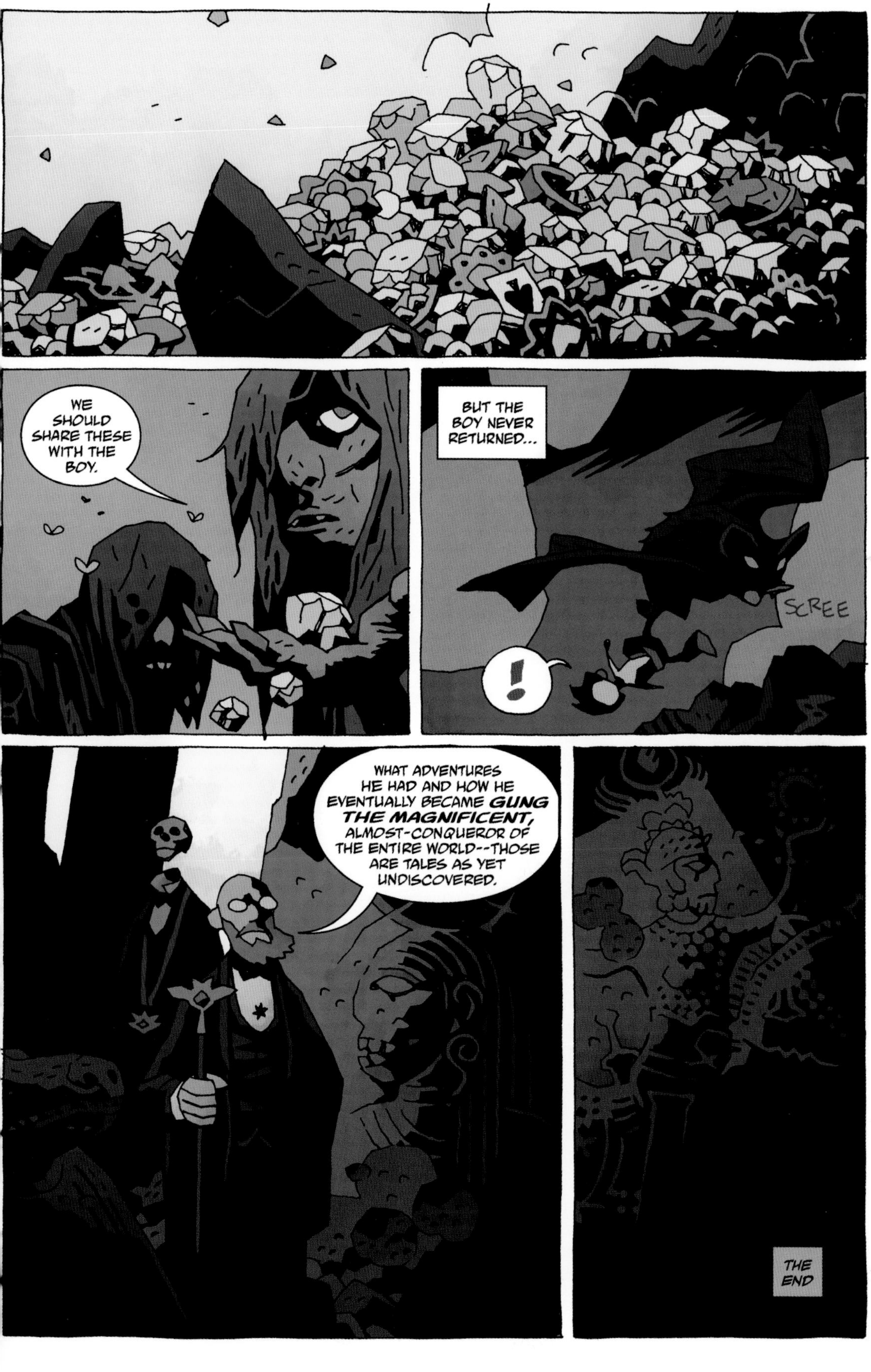

WE SHOULD SHARE THESE WITH THE BOY.
BUT THE BOY NEVER RETURNED...
SCREE
!
WHAT ADVENTURES HE HAD AND HOW HE EVENTUALLY BECAME **GUNG THE MAGNIFICENT,** ALMOST-CONQUEROR OF THE ENTIRE WORLD--THOSE ARE TALES AS YET UNDISCOVERED.
THE END

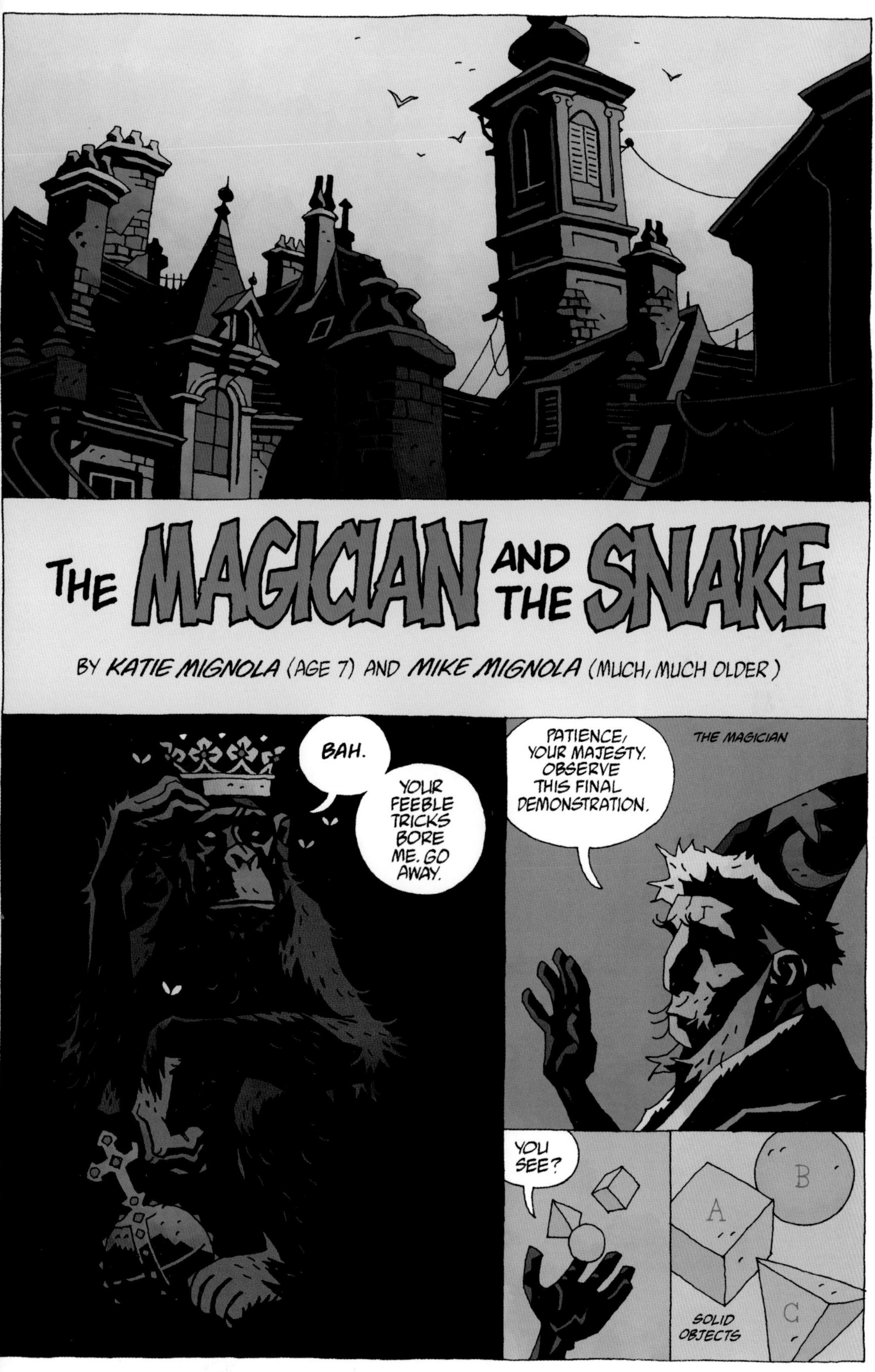
THE MAGICIAN AND THE SNAKE
BY KATIE MIGNOLA (AGE 7) AND MIKE MIGNOLA (MUCH, MUCH OLDER)
BAH.
YOUR FEEBLE TRICKS BORE ME. GO AWAY.
THE MAGICIAN
PATIENCE, YOUR MAJESTY. OBSERVE THIS FINAL DEMONSTRATION.
YOU SEE?
A
B
C
SOLID OBJECTS

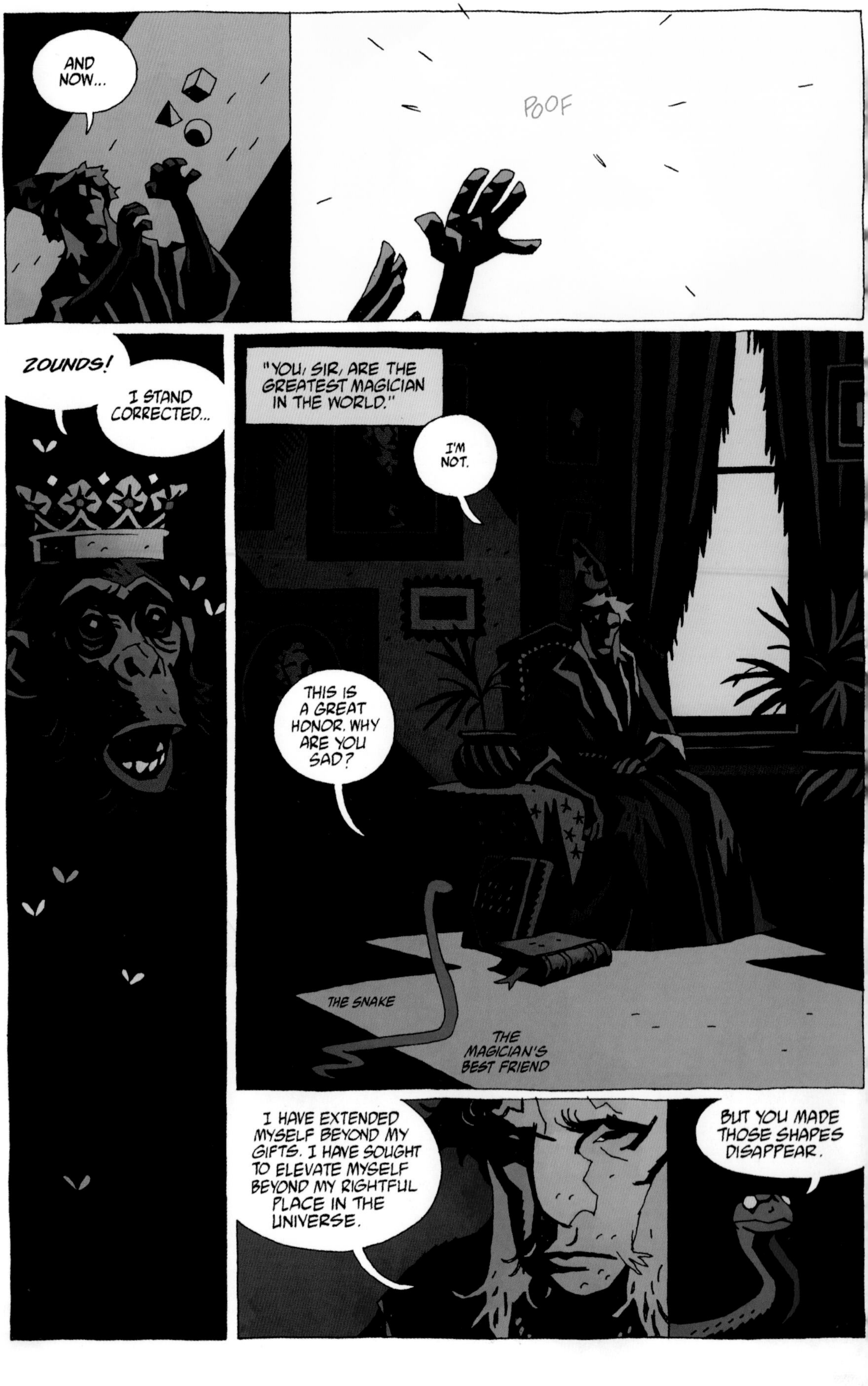
AND NOW...
POOF
ZOUNDS!
I STAND CORRECTED...
"YOU, SIR, ARE THE GREATEST MAGICIAN IN THE WORLD."
I'M NOT.
THIS IS A GREAT HONOR. WHY ARE YOU SAD?
THE SNAKE
THE MAGICIAN'S BEST FRIEND
I HAVE EXTENDED MYSELF BEYOND MY GIFTS. I HAVE SOUGHT TO ELEVATE MYSELF BEYOND MY RIGHTFUL PLACE IN THE UNIVERSE.
BUT YOU MADE THOSE SHAPES DISAPPEAR.

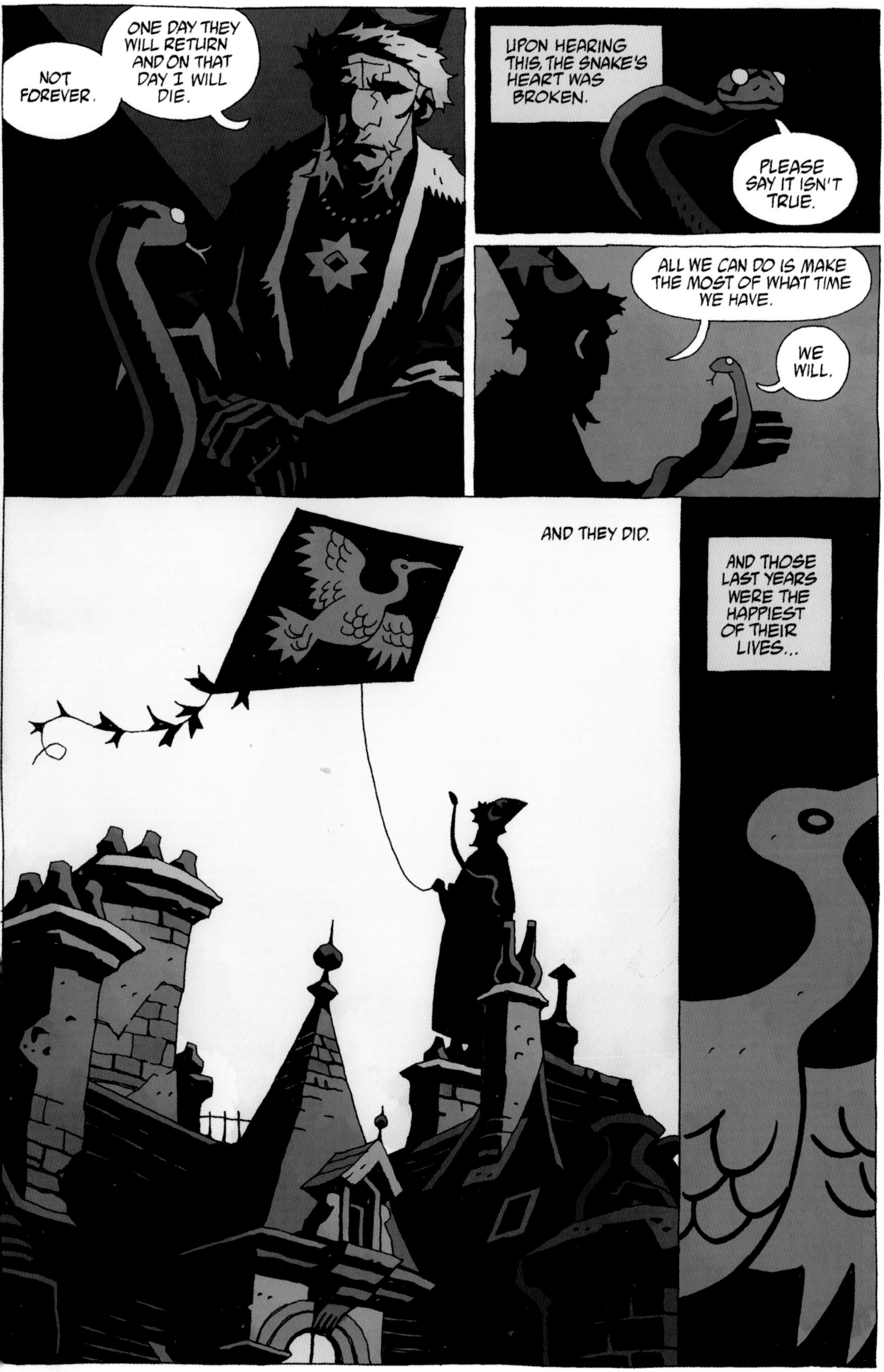
NOT FOREVER.
ONE DAY THEY WILL RETURN AND ON THAT DAY I WILL DIE.
UPON HEARING THIS, THE SNAKE'S HEART WAS BROKEN.
PLEASE SAY IT ISN'T TRUE.
ALL WE CAN DO IS MAKE THE MOST OF WHAT TIME WE HAVE.
WE WILL.
AND THEY DID.
AND THOSE LAST YEARS WERE THE HAPPIEST OF THEIR LIVES...

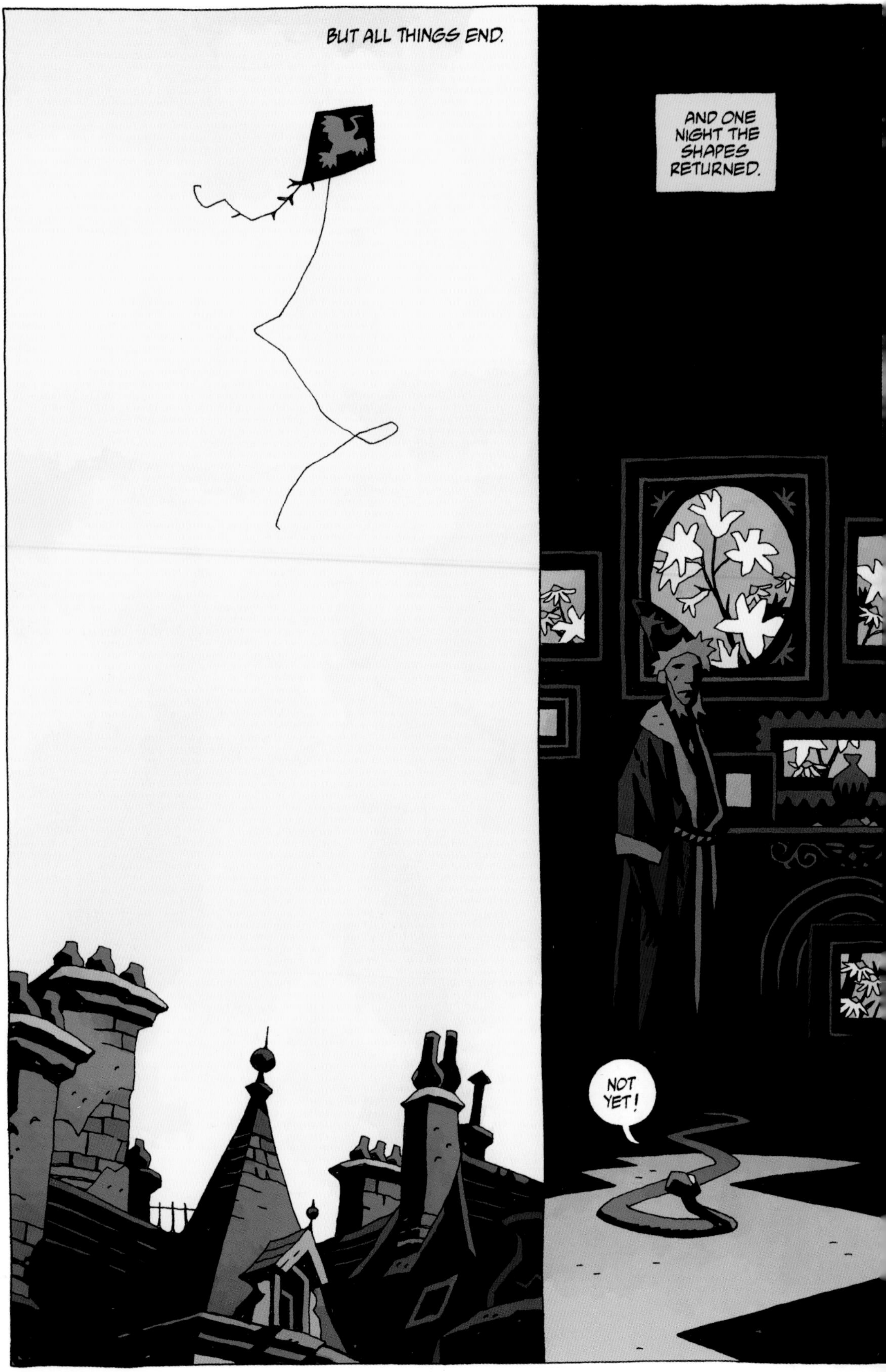

BUT ALL THINGS END.
AND ONE NIGHT THE SHAPES RETURNED.
NOT YET!

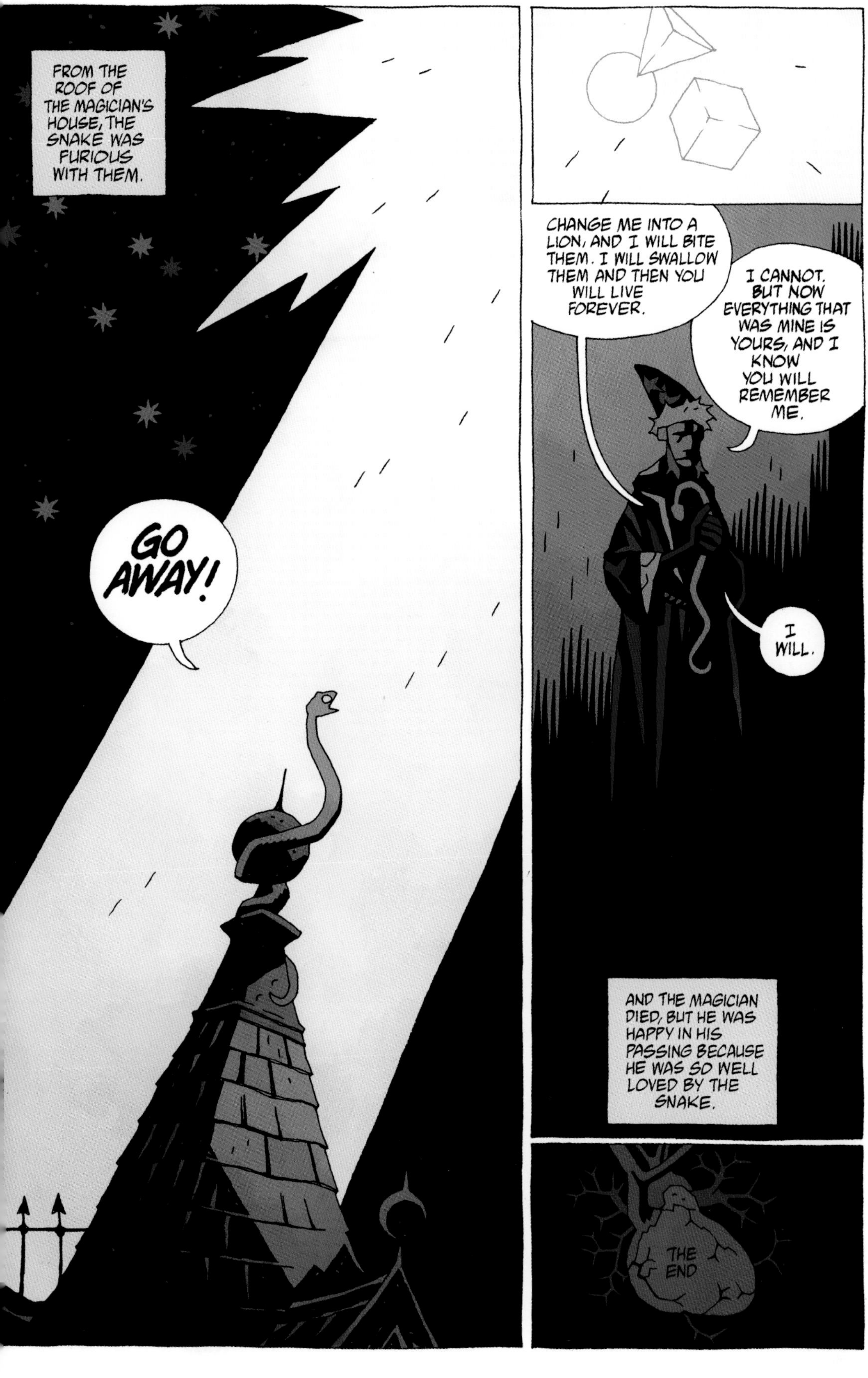
FROM THE ROOF OF THE MAGICIAN'S HOUSE, THE SNAKE WAS FURIOUS WITH THEM.
GO AWAY!
CHANGE ME INTO A LION, AND I WILL BITE THEM. I WILL SWALLOW THEM AND THEN YOU WILL LIVE FOREVER.
I CANNOT. BUT NOW EVERYTHING THAT WAS MINE IS YOURS, AND I KNOW YOU WILL REMEMBER ME.
I WILL.
AND THE MAGICIAN DIED, BUT HE WAS HAPPY IN HIS PASSING BECAUSE HE WAS SO WELL LOVED BY THE SNAKE.
THE END

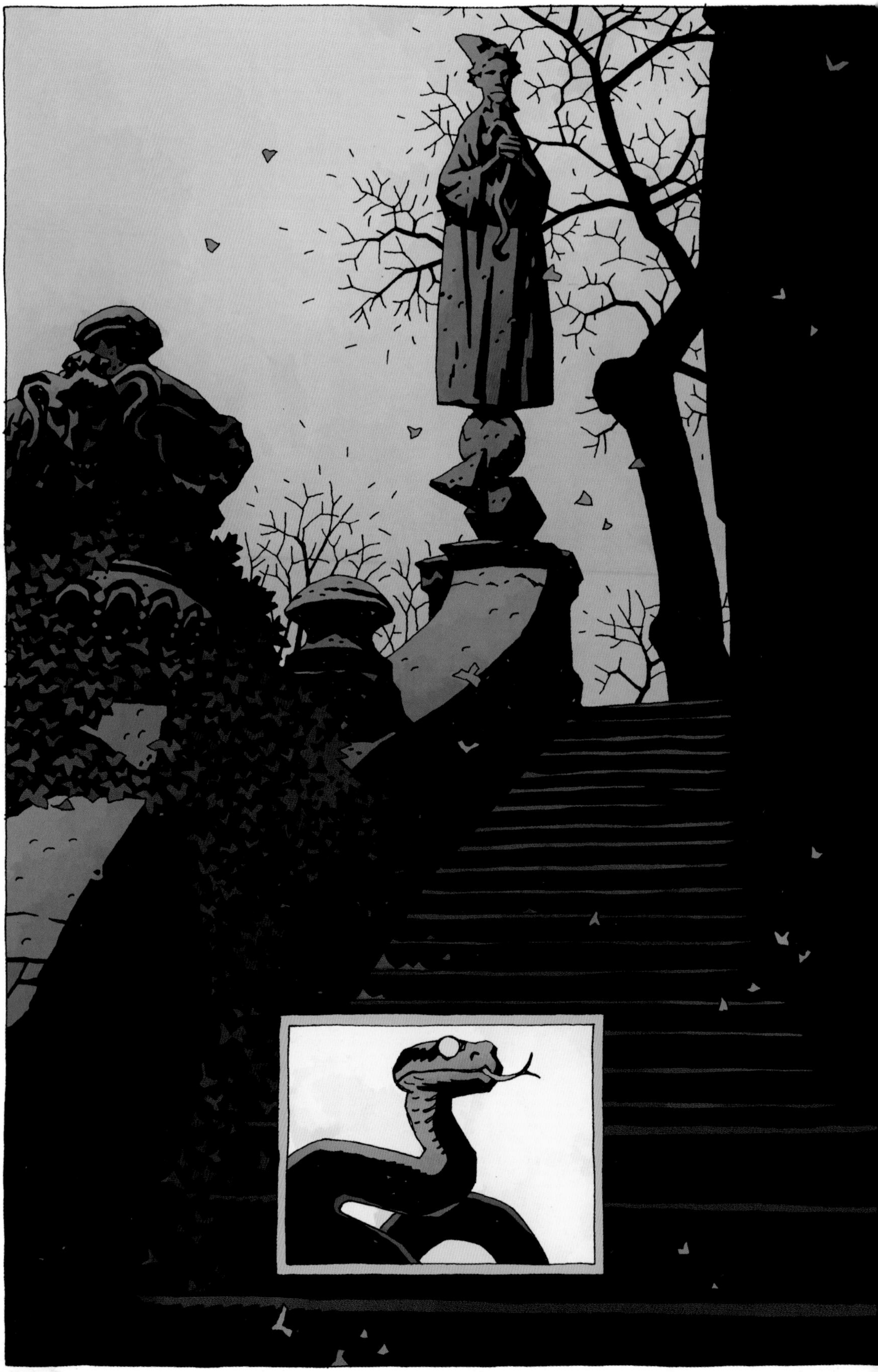

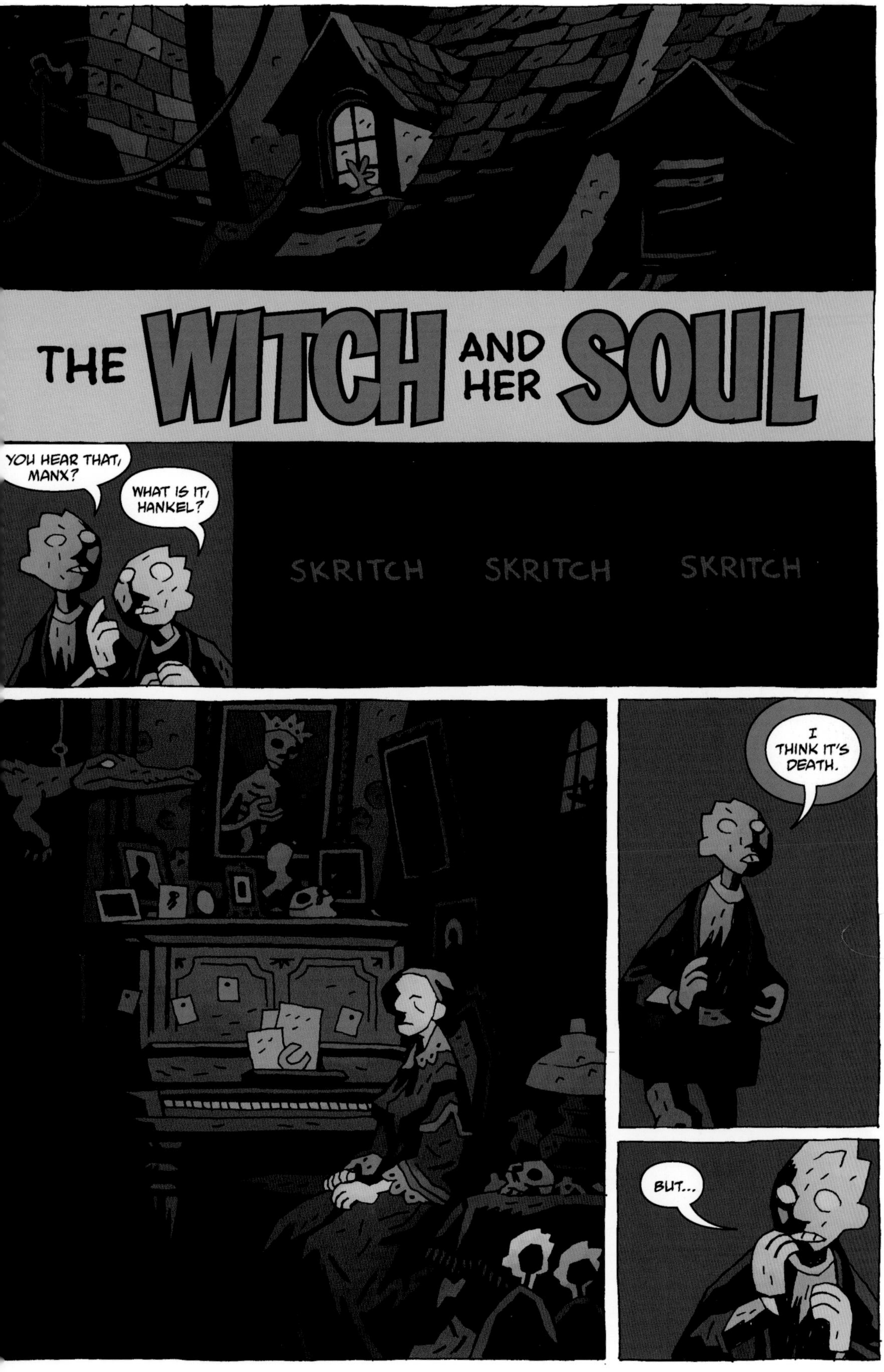
THE WITCH AND HER SOUL
YOU HEAR THAT, MANX?
WHAT IS IT, HANKEL?
SKRITCH SKRITCH SKRITCH
I THINK IT'S DEATH.
BUT...

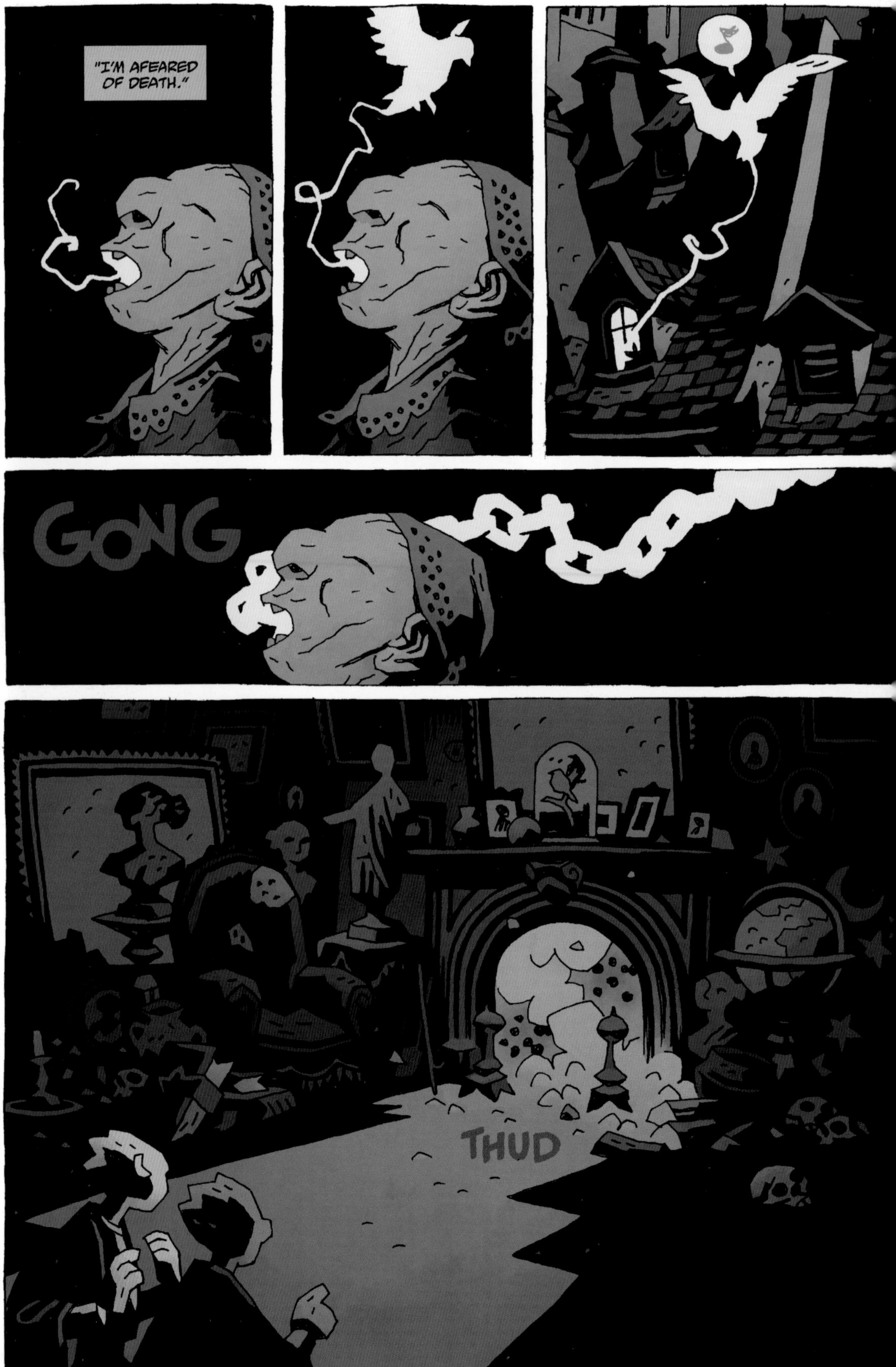
"I'M AFEARED OF DEATH."
GONG
THUD

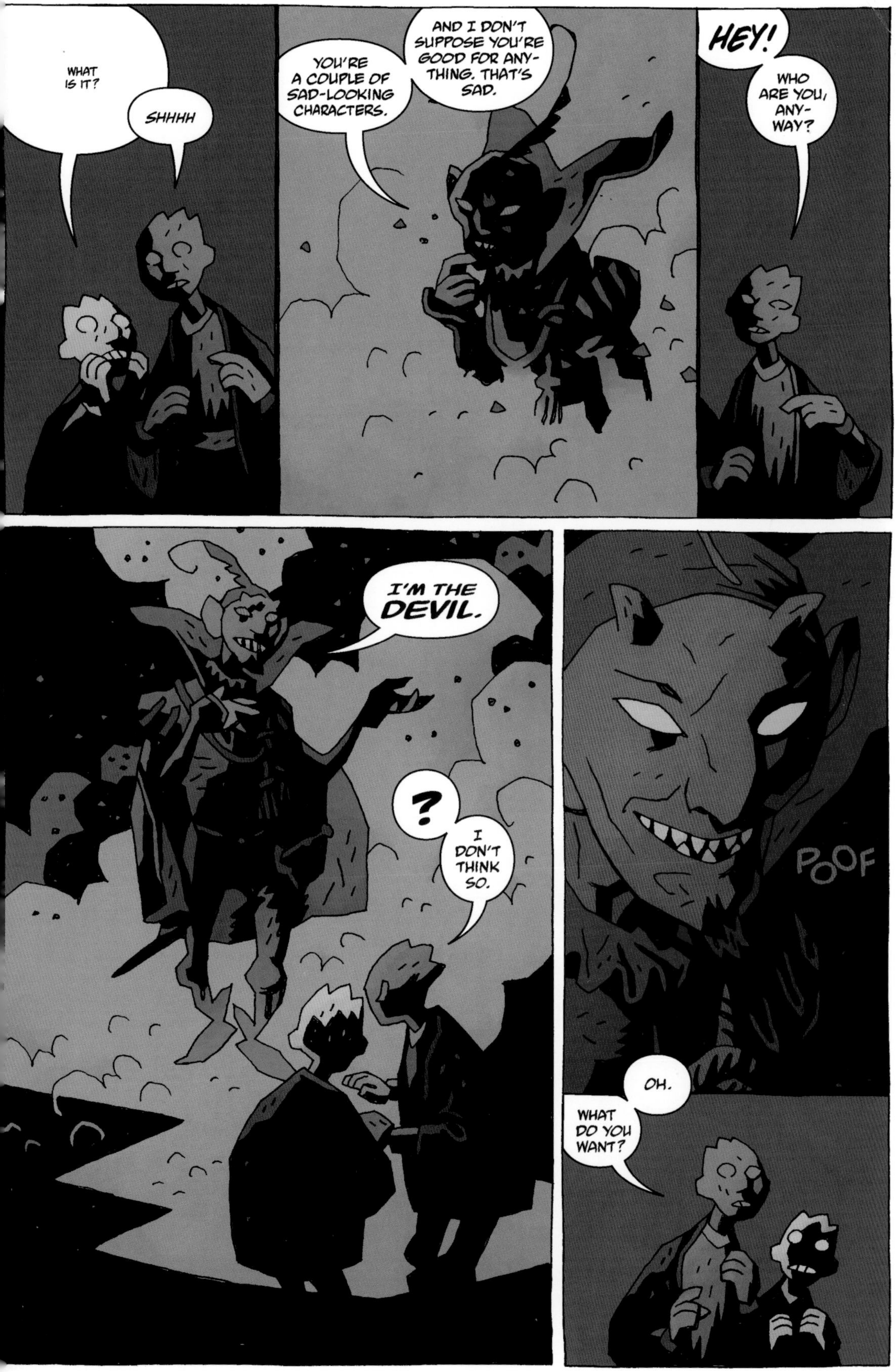
WHAT IS IT?
SHHHH
YOU'RE A COUPLE OF SAD-LOOKING CHARACTERS.
AND I DON'T SUPPOSE YOU'RE GOOD FOR ANY-THING. THAT'S SAD.
HEY!
WHO ARE YOU, ANY-WAY?
I'M THE DEVIL.
?
I DON'T THINK SO.
POOF
OH.
WHAT DO YOU WANT?

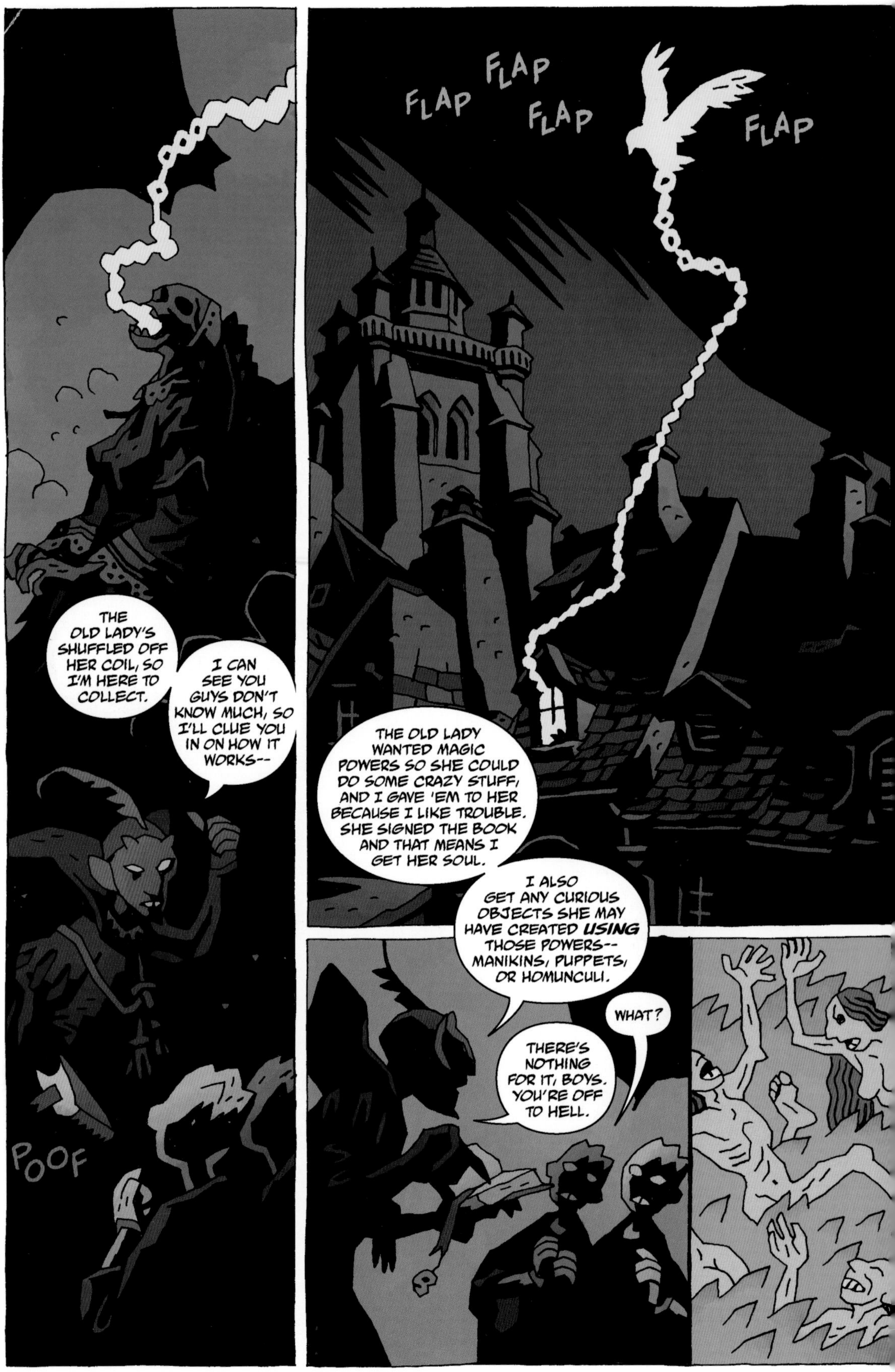
THE OLD LADY'S SHUFFLED OFF HER COIL, SO I'M HERE TO COLLECT.
I CAN SEE YOU GUYS DON'T KNOW MUCH, SO I'LL CLUE YOU IN ON HOW IT WORKS--
POOF
FLAP FLAP FLAP FLAP
THE OLD LADY WANTED MAGIC POWERS SO SHE COULD DO SOME CRAZY STUFF, AND I GAVE 'EM TO HER BECAUSE I LIKE TROUBLE. SHE SIGNED THE BOOK AND THAT MEANS I GET HER SOUL.
I ALSO GET ANY CURIOUS OBJECTS SHE MAY HAVE CREATED **USING** THOSE POWERS-- MANIKINS, PUPPETS, OR HOMUNCULI.
WHAT?
THERE'S NOTHING FOR IT, BOYS. YOU'RE OFF TO HELL.

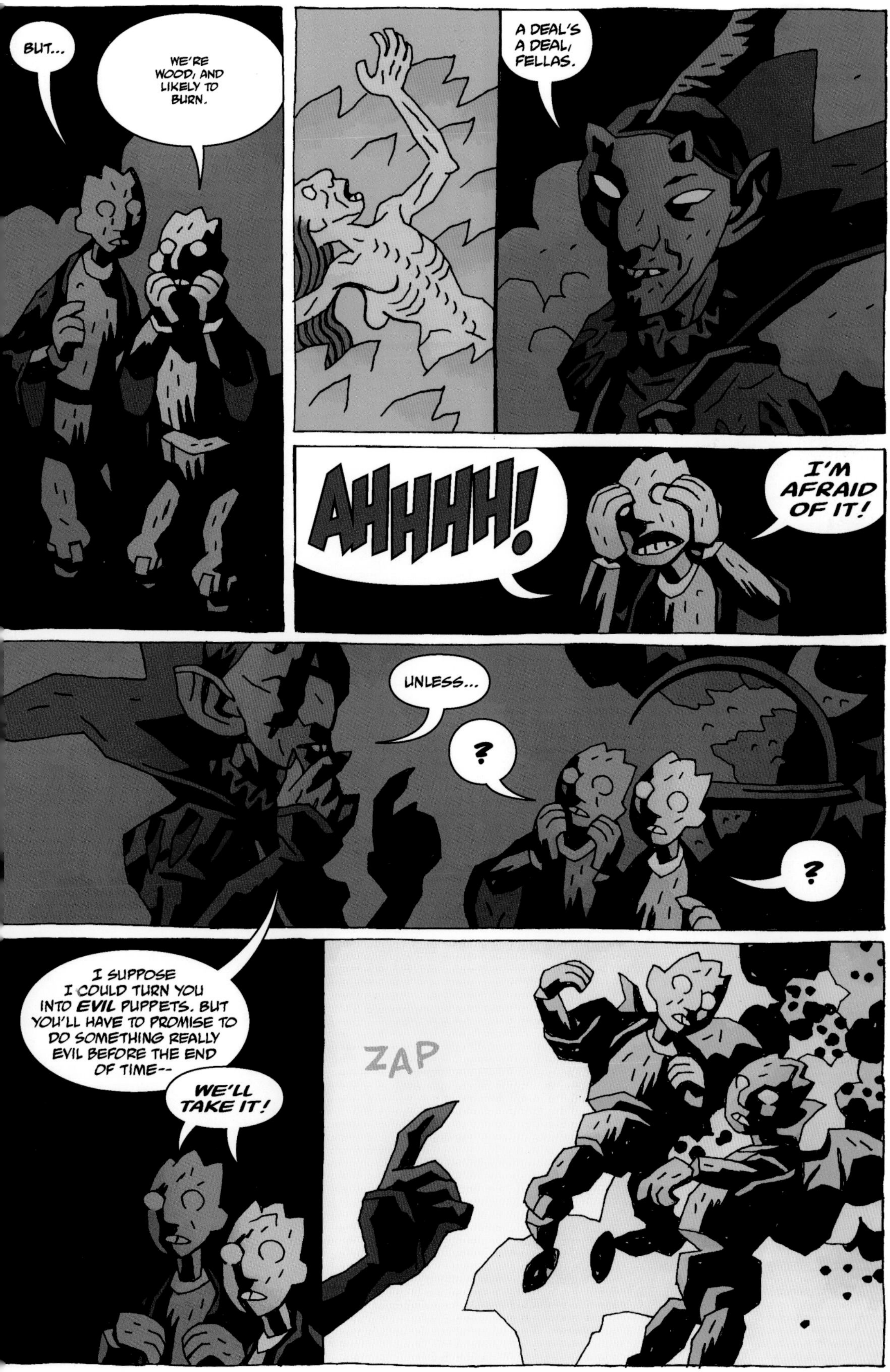
BUT...
WE'RE WOOD, AND LIKELY TO BURN.
A DEAL'S A DEAL, FELLAS.
AHHHH!
I'M AFRAID OF IT!
UNLESS...
?
?
I SUPPOSE I COULD TURN YOU INTO EVIL PUPPETS. BUT YOU'LL HAVE TO PROMISE TO DO SOMETHING REALLY EVIL BEFORE THE END OF TIME--
WE'LL TAKE IT!
ZAP

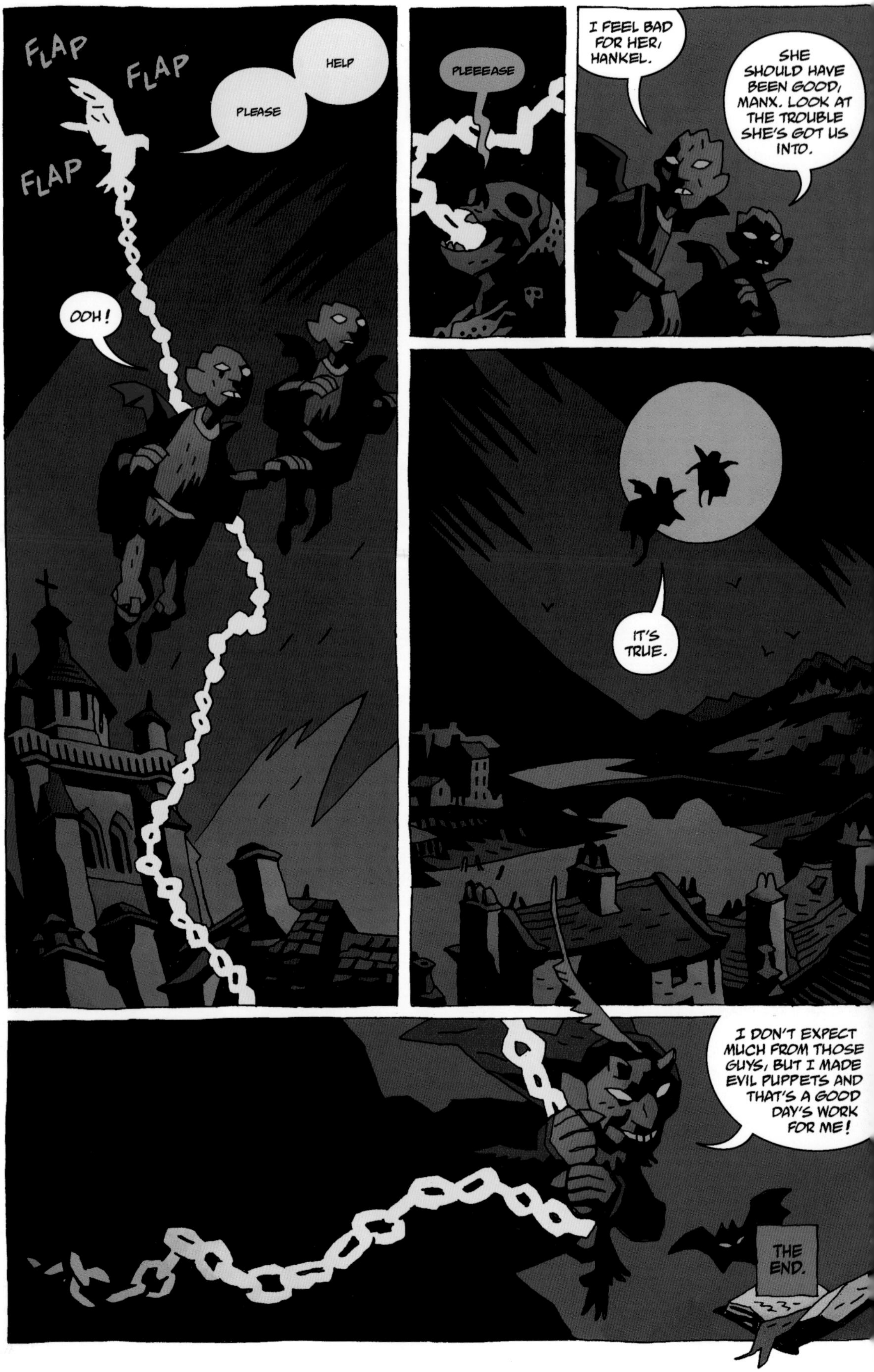

FLAP
FLAP
FLAP
PLEASE
HELP
OOH!
PLEEEASE
I FEEL BAD FOR HER, HANKEL.
SHE SHOULD HAVE BEEN GOOD, MANX. LOOK AT THE TROUBLE SHE'S GOT US INTO.
IT'S TRUE.
I DON'T EXPECT MUCH FROM THOSE GUYS, BUT I MADE EVIL PUPPETS AND THAT'S A GOOD DAY'S WORK FOR ME!
THE END.

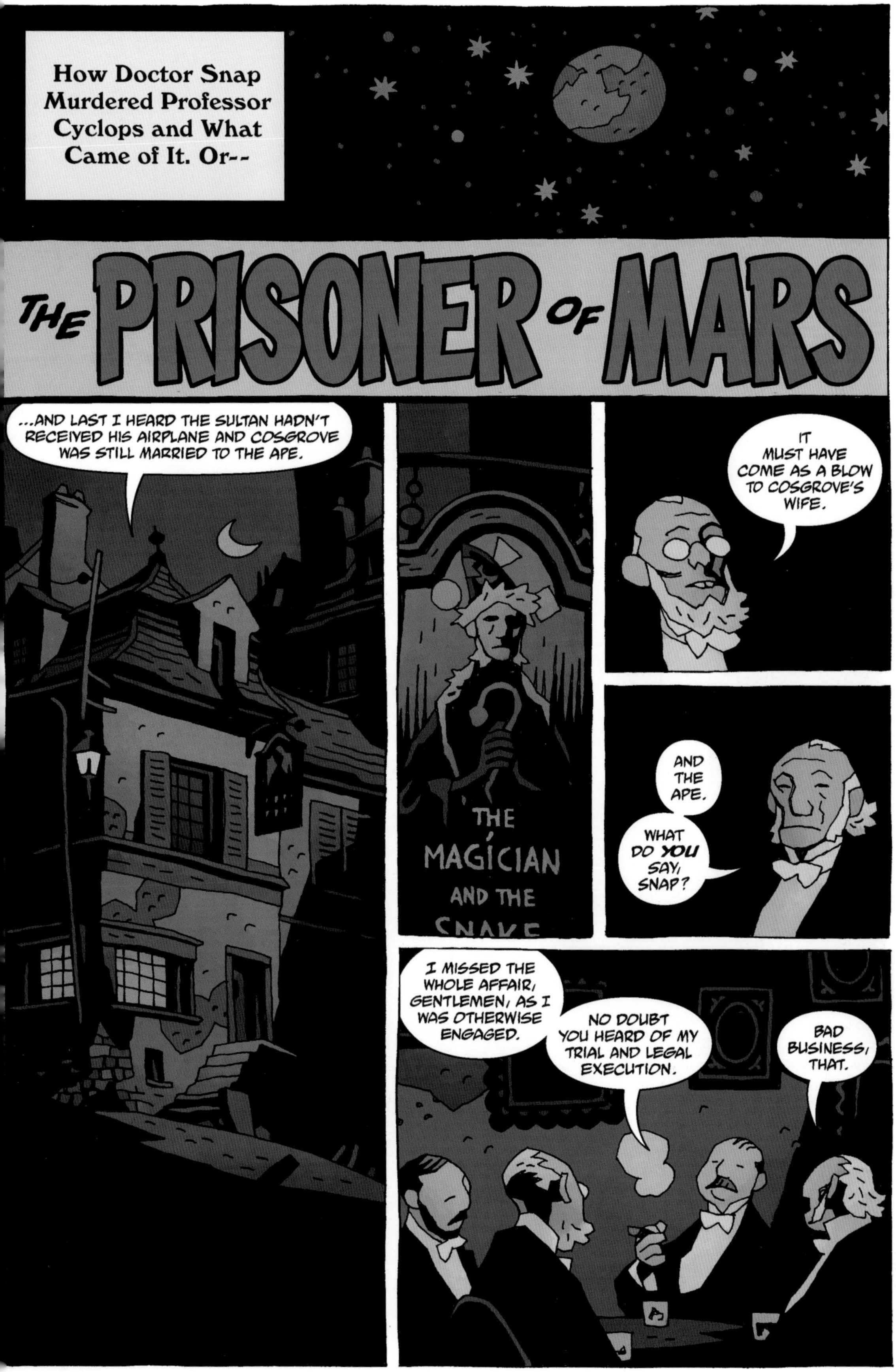
How Doctor Snap Murdered Professor Cyclops and What Came of It. Or--
THE PRISONER OF MARS
...AND LAST I HEARD THE SULTAN HADN'T RECEIVED HIS AIRPLANE AND COSGROVE WAS STILL MARRIED TO THE APE.
THE MAGICIAN AND THE SNAKE
IT MUST HAVE COME AS A BLOW TO COSGROVE'S WIFE.
AND THE APE.
WHAT DO YOU SAY, SNAP?
I MISSED THE WHOLE AFFAIR, GENTLEMEN, AS I WAS OTHERWISE ENGAGED.
NO DOUBT YOU HEARD OF MY TRIAL AND LEGAL EXECUTION.
BAD BUSINESS, THAT.

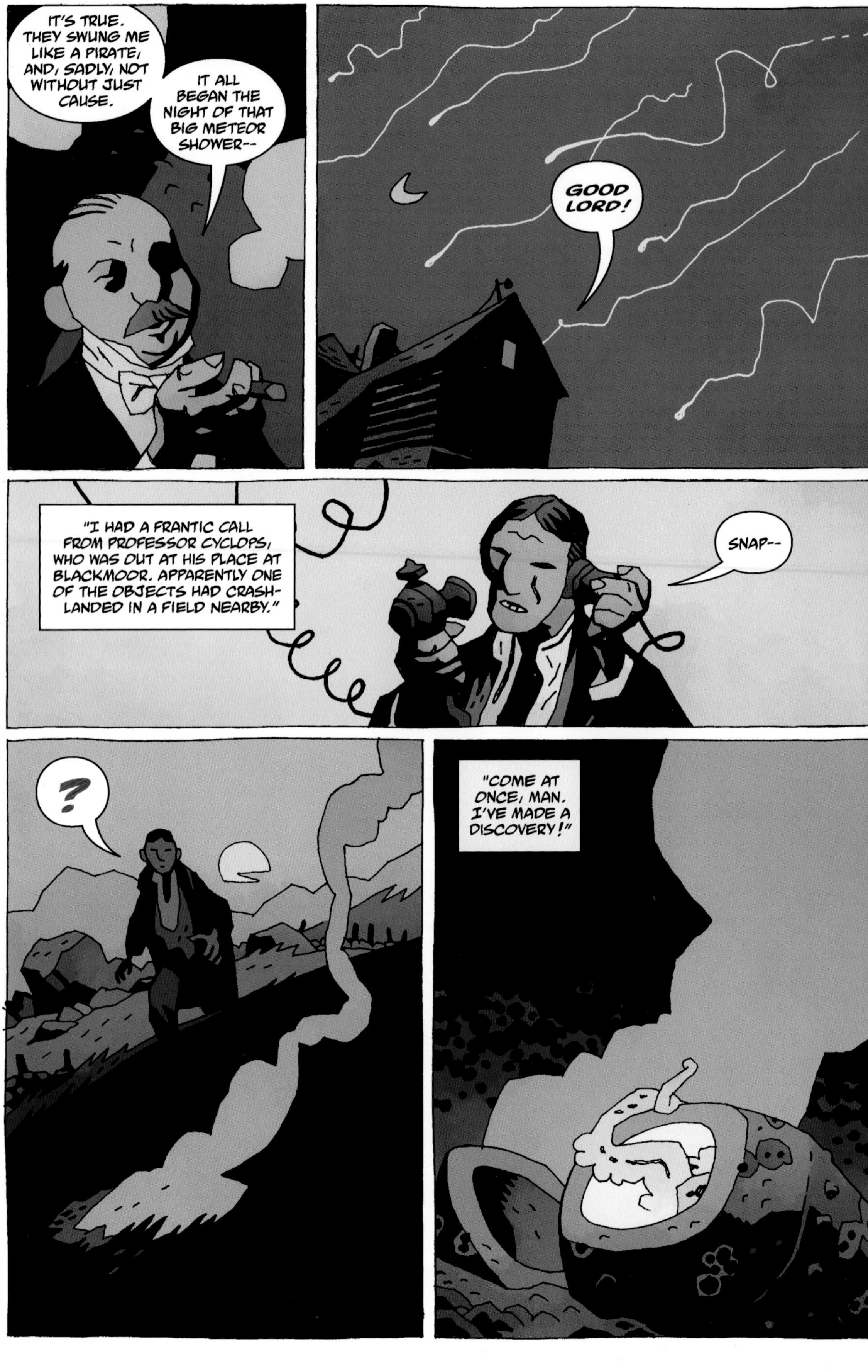
IT'S TRUE. THEY SWUNG ME LIKE A PIRATE, AND, SADLY, NOT WITHOUT JUST CAUSE.
IT ALL BEGAN THE NIGHT OF THAT BIG METEOR SHOWER--
GOOD LORD!
"I HAD A FRANTIC CALL FROM PROFESSOR CYCLOPS, WHO WAS OUT AT HIS PLACE AT BLACKMOOR. APPARENTLY ONE OF THE OBJECTS HAD CRASH-LANDED IN A FIELD NEARBY."
SNAP--
?
"COME AT ONCE, MAN. I'VE MADE A DISCOVERY!"

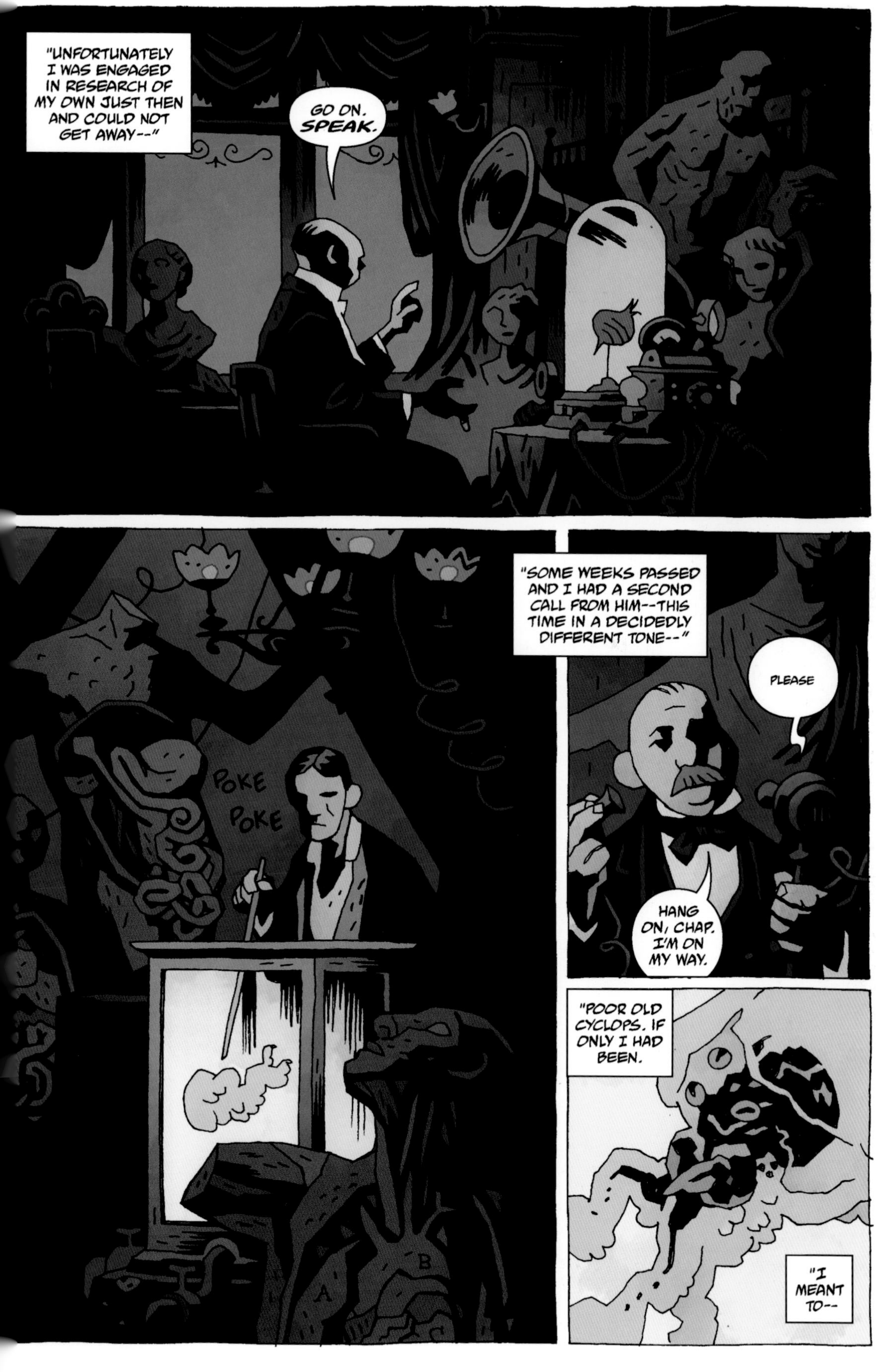
"UNFORTUNATELY I WAS ENGAGED IN RESEARCH OF MY OWN JUST THEN AND COULD NOT GET AWAY--"
GO ON. SPEAK.
POKE
POKE
"SOME WEEKS PASSED AND I HAD A SECOND CALL FROM HIM--THIS TIME IN A DECIDEDLY DIFFERENT TONE--"
PLEASE
HANG ON, CHAP. I'M ON MY WAY.
"POOR OLD CYCLOPS. IF ONLY I HAD BEEN.
"I MEANT TO--

"BUT ONCE AGAIN I'D BECOME DISTRACTED AND WAS SEVERAL DAYS LATE ARRIVING."

HELLO?

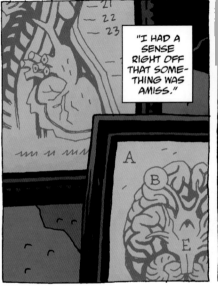

"I HAD A SENSE RIGHT OFF THAT SOMETHING WAS AMISS."

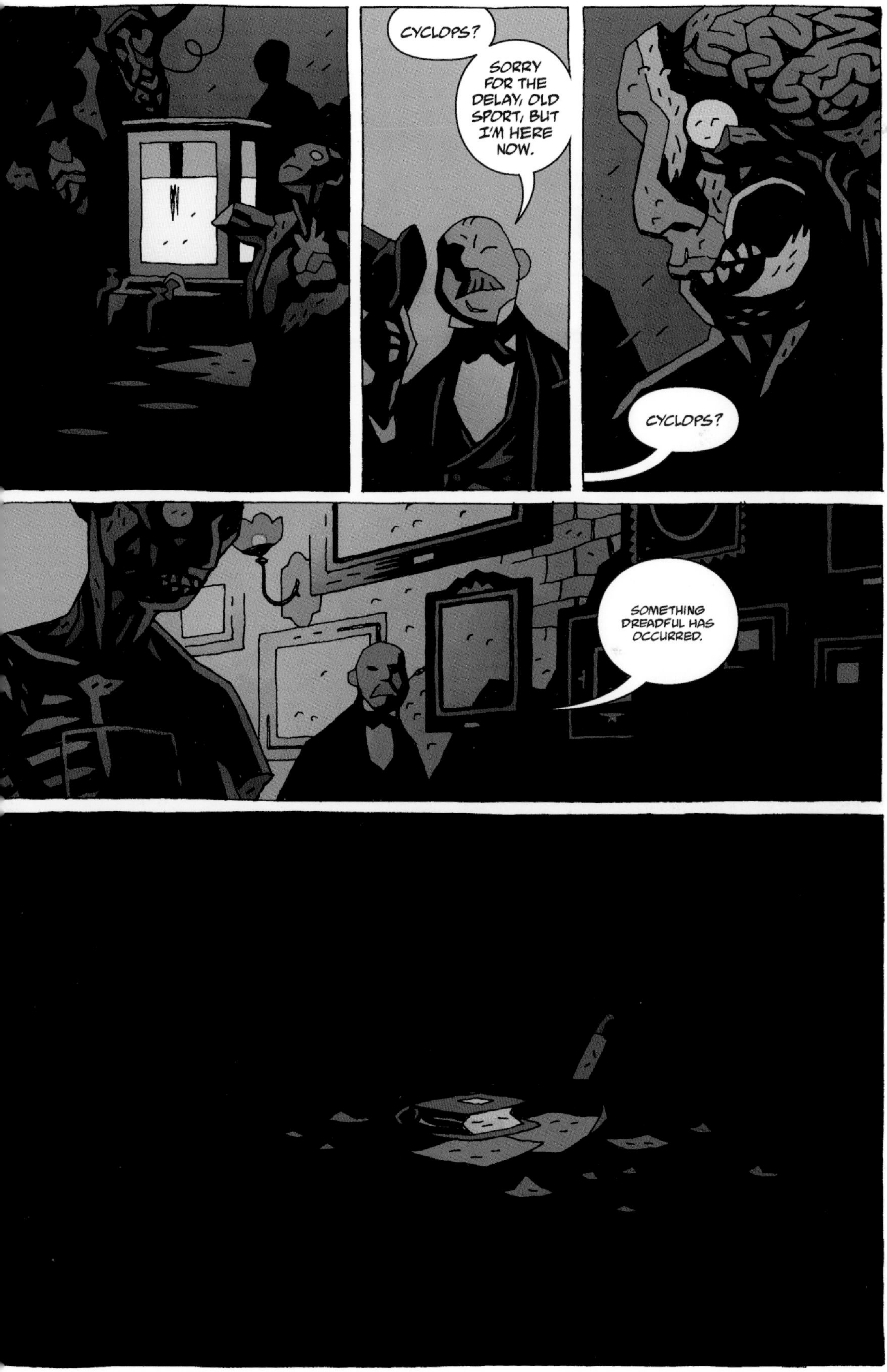
CYCLOPS?
SORRY FOR THE DELAY, OLD SPORT, BUT I'M HERE NOW.
CYCLOPS?
SOMETHING DREADFUL HAS OCCURRED.

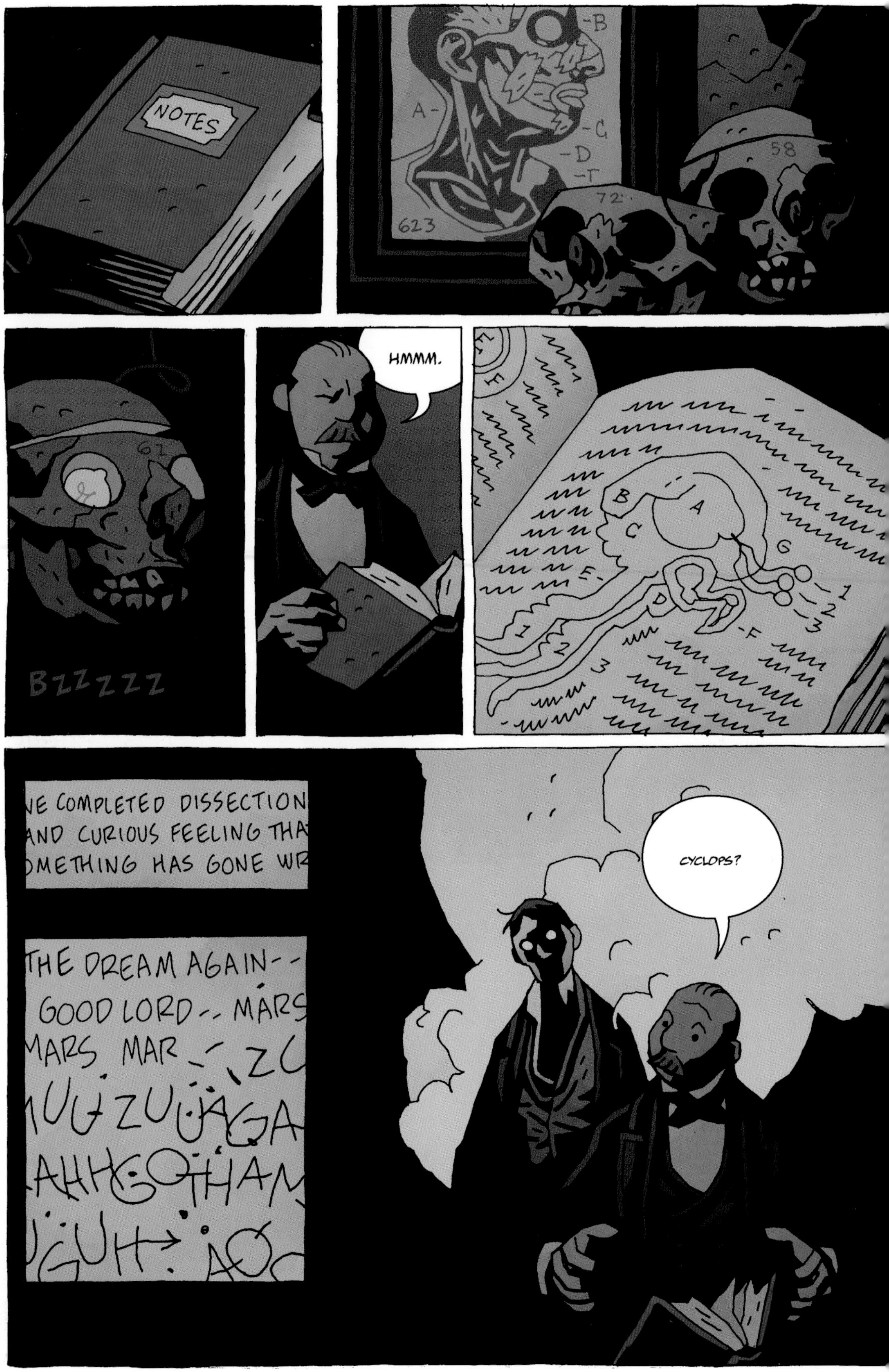
NOTES
A-
-B
-C
-D
-T
623
72
58
61
BZZZZZZ
HMMM.
A
B
C
D
E
F
G
1
2
3
WE COMPLETED DISSECTION
AND CURIOUS FEELING THA
OMETHING HAS GONE WR
THE DREAM AGAIN--
GOOD LORD-- MARS
MARS MAR
CYCLOPS?

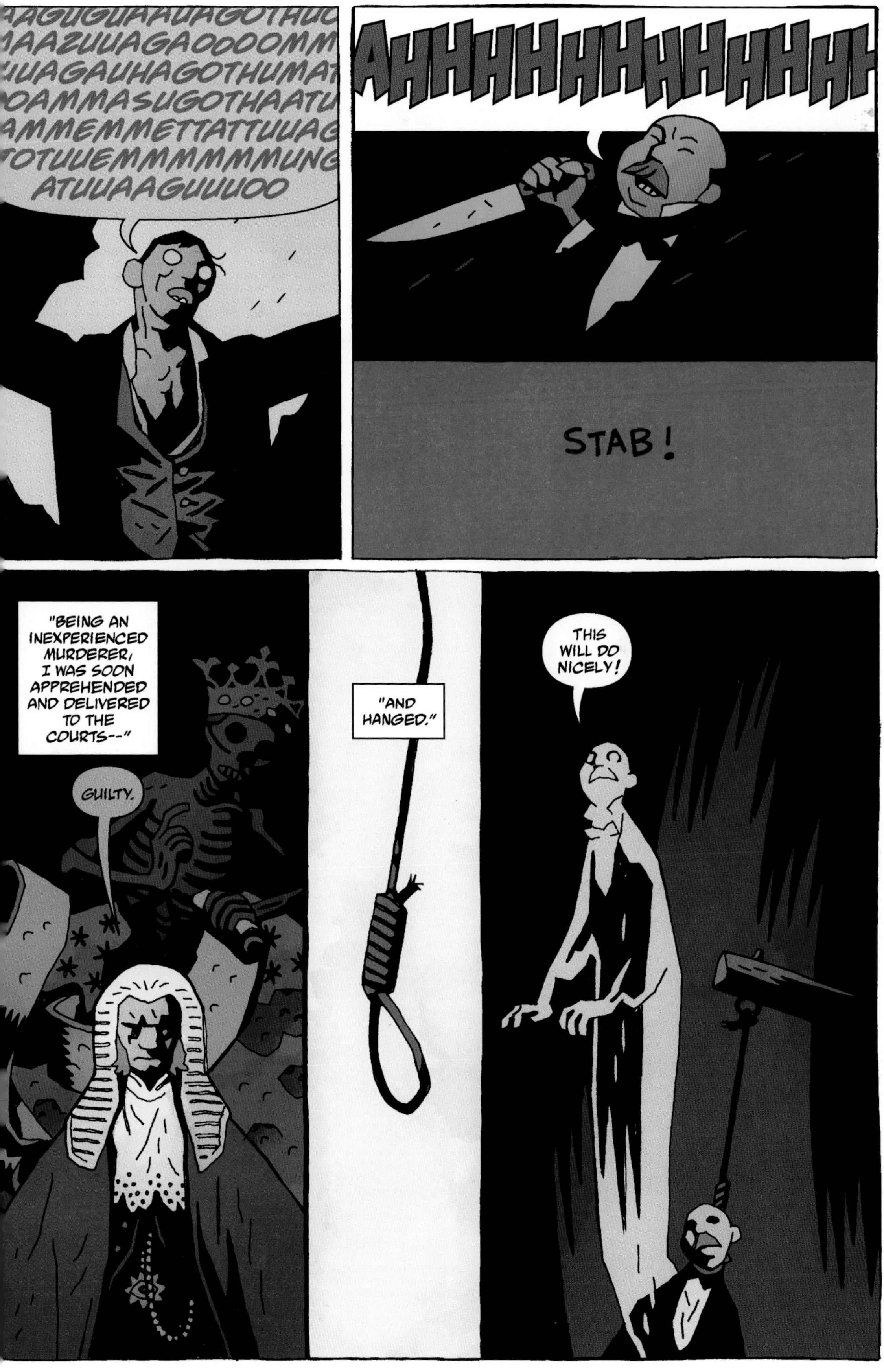
AAGUGUAAUAGOTHUC MAAZUUAGAOOOOMM UUAGAUHAGOTHUMAT OAMMASUGOTHAATU AMMEMMETTATTUUAG OTUUEMMMMMMUNG ATUUAAGUUUOO
AHHHHHHHHHHHH
STAB!
"BEING AN INEXPERIENCED MURDERER, I WAS SOON APPREHENDED AND DELIVERED TO THE COURTS--"
GUILTY.
"AND HANGED."
THIS WILL DO NICELY!

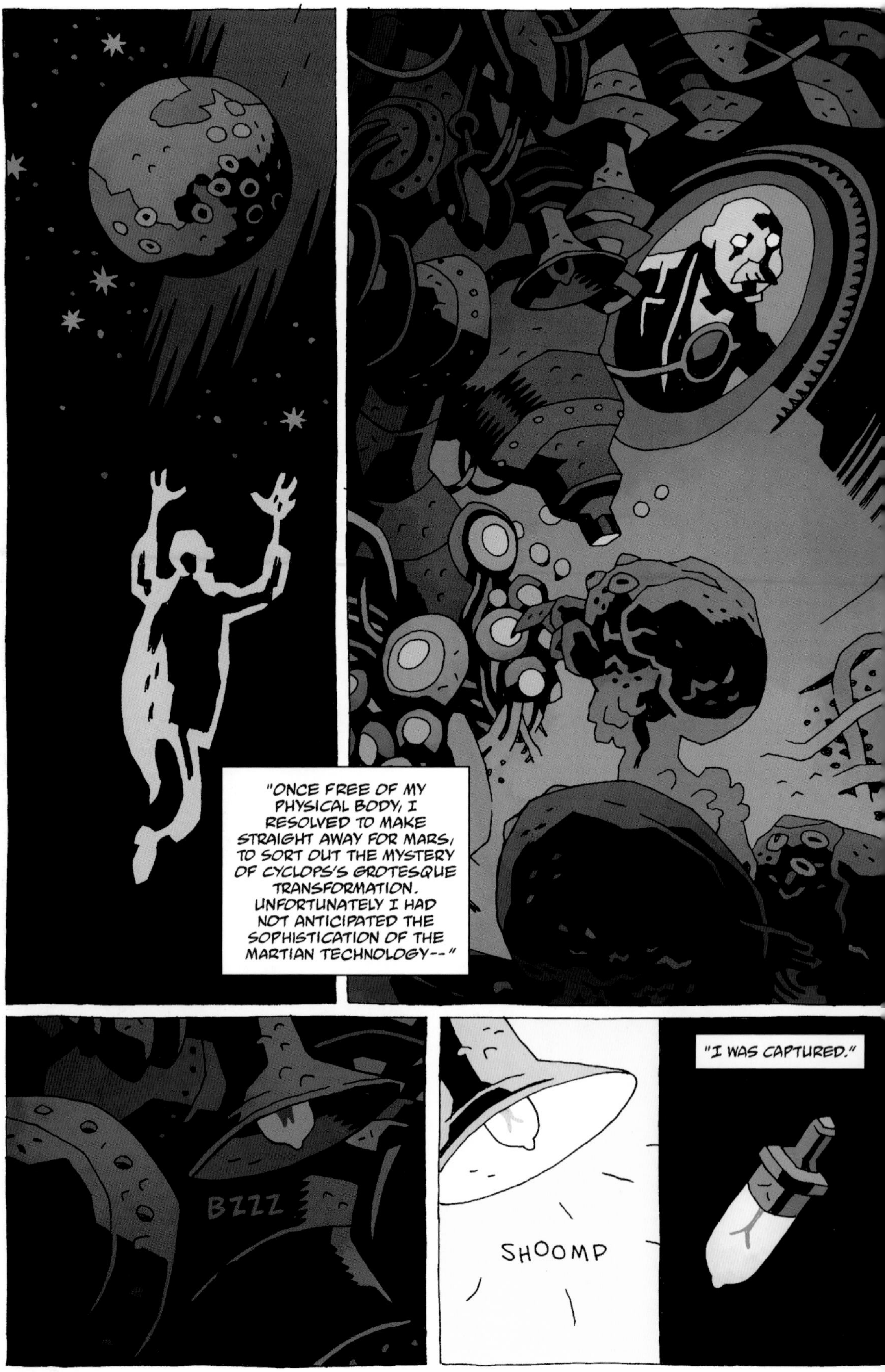

"ONCE FREE OF MY PHYSICAL BODY, I RESOLVED TO MAKE STRAIGHT AWAY FOR MARS, TO SORT OUT THE MYSTERY OF CYCLOPS'S GROTESQUE TRANSFORMATION. UNFORTUNATELY I HAD NOT ANTICIPATED THE SOPHISTICATION OF THE MARTIAN TECHNOLOGY--"
BZZZ
SHOOMP
"I WAS CAPTURED."

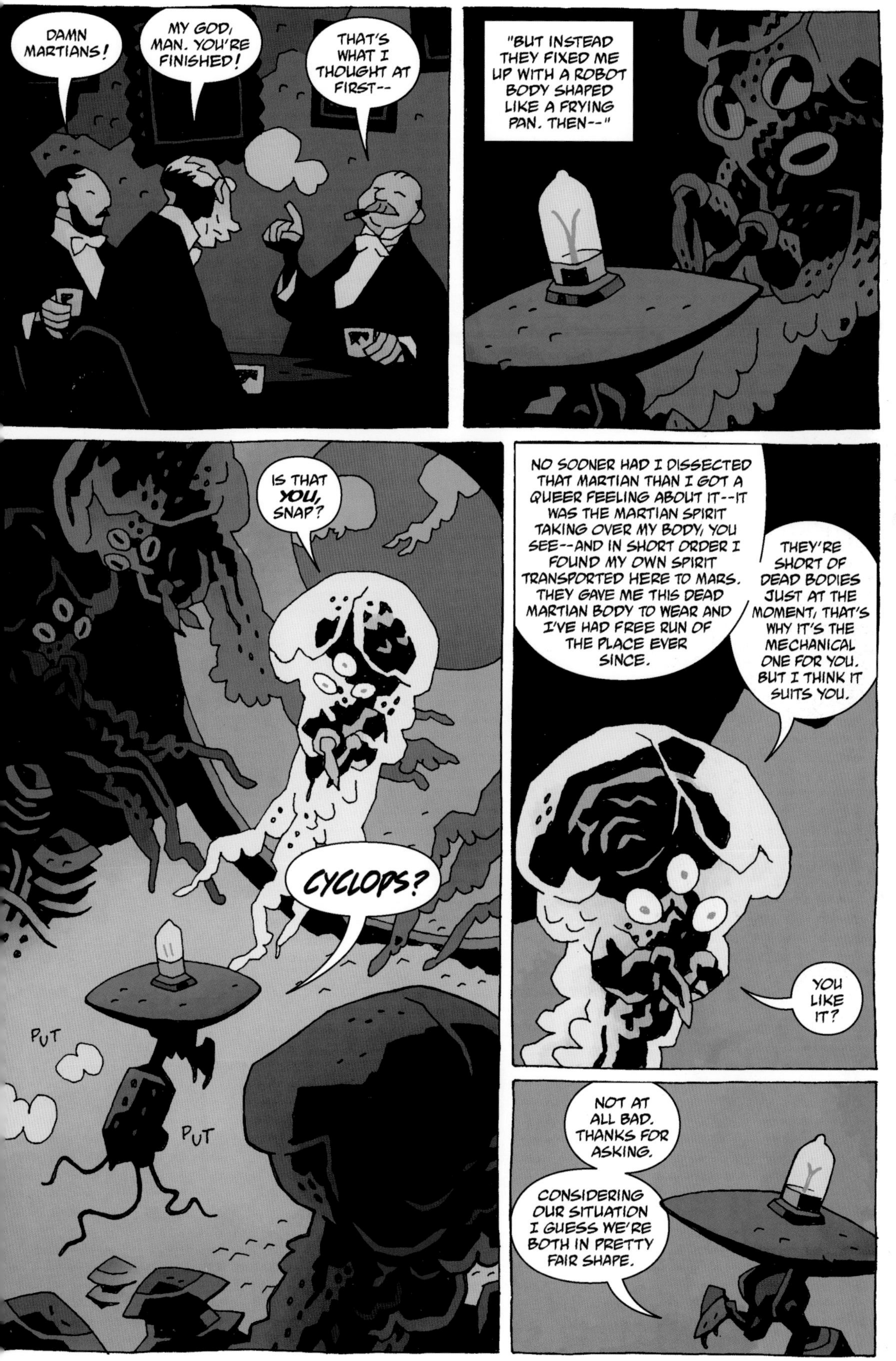

DAMN MARTIANS!
MY GOD, MAN. YOU'RE FINISHED!
THAT'S WHAT I THOUGHT AT FIRST--
"BUT INSTEAD THEY FIXED ME UP WITH A ROBOT BODY SHAPED LIKE A FRYING PAN. THEN--"
IS THAT YOU, SNAP?
CYCLOPS?
PUT
PUT
NO SOONER HAD I DISSECTED THAT MARTIAN THAN I GOT A QUEER FEELING ABOUT IT--IT WAS THE MARTIAN SPIRIT TAKING OVER MY BODY, YOU SEE--AND IN SHORT ORDER I FOUND MY OWN SPIRIT TRANSPORTED HERE TO MARS. THEY GAVE ME THIS DEAD MARTIAN BODY TO WEAR AND I'VE HAD FREE RUN OF THE PLACE EVER SINCE.
THEY'RE SHORT OF DEAD BODIES JUST AT THE MOMENT, THAT'S WHY IT'S THE MECHANICAL ONE FOR YOU. BUT I THINK IT SUITS YOU.
YOU LIKE IT?
NOT AT ALL BAD. THANKS FOR ASKING.
CONSIDERING OUR SITUATION I GUESS WE'RE BOTH IN PRETTY FAIR SHAPE.

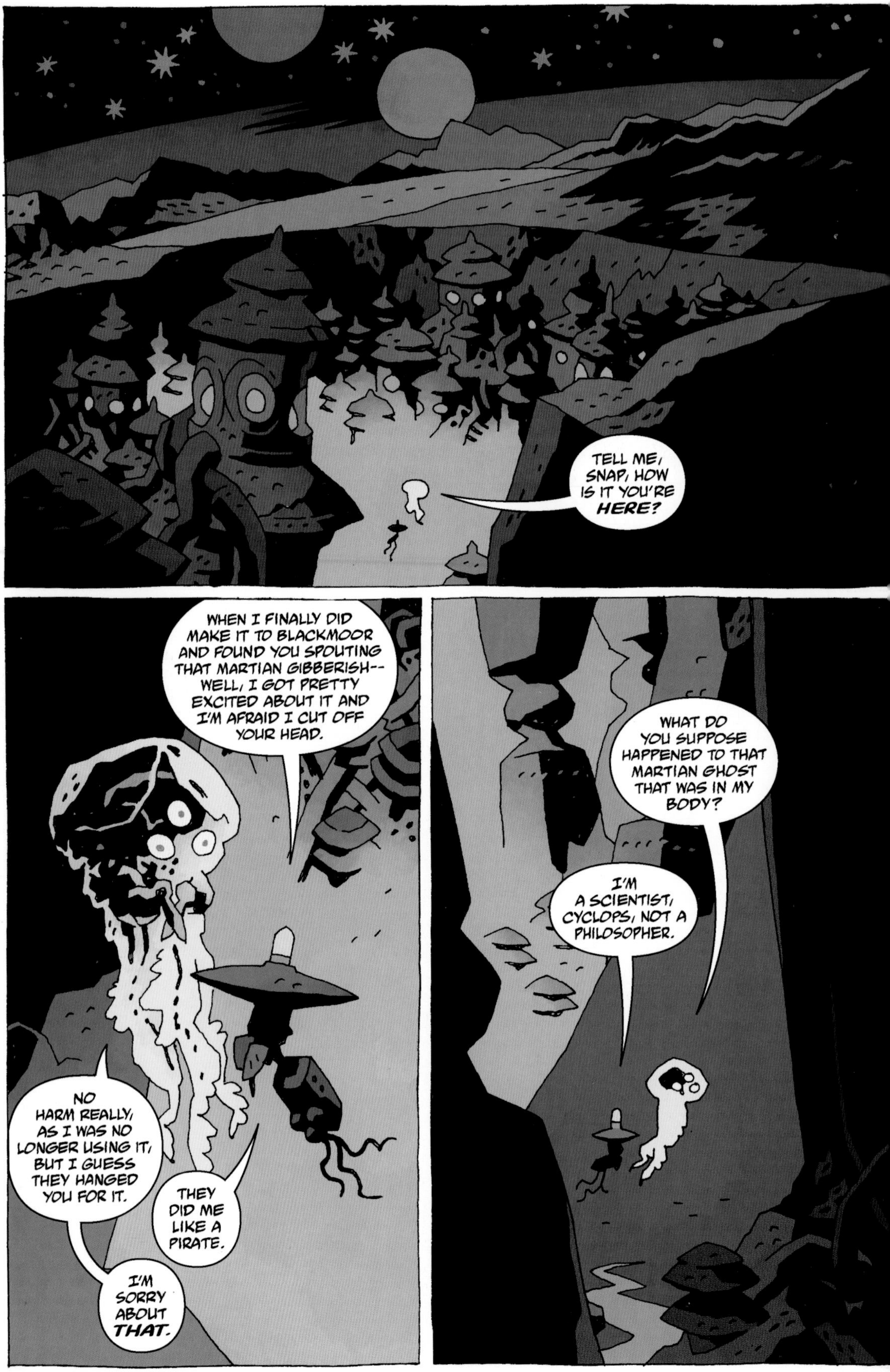
TELL ME, SNAP, HOW IS IT YOU'RE HERE?
WHEN I FINALLY DID MAKE IT TO BLACKMOOR AND FOUND YOU SPOUTING THAT MARTIAN GIBBERISH-- WELL, I GOT PRETTY EXCITED ABOUT IT AND I'M AFRAID I CUT OFF YOUR HEAD.
NO HARM REALLY, AS I WAS NO LONGER USING IT, BUT I GUESS THEY HANGED YOU FOR IT.
THEY DID ME LIKE A PIRATE.
I'M SORRY ABOUT THAT.
WHAT DO YOU SUPPOSE HAPPENED TO THAT MARTIAN GHOST THAT WAS IN MY BODY?
I'M A SCIENTIST, CYCLOPS, NOT A PHILOSOPHER.

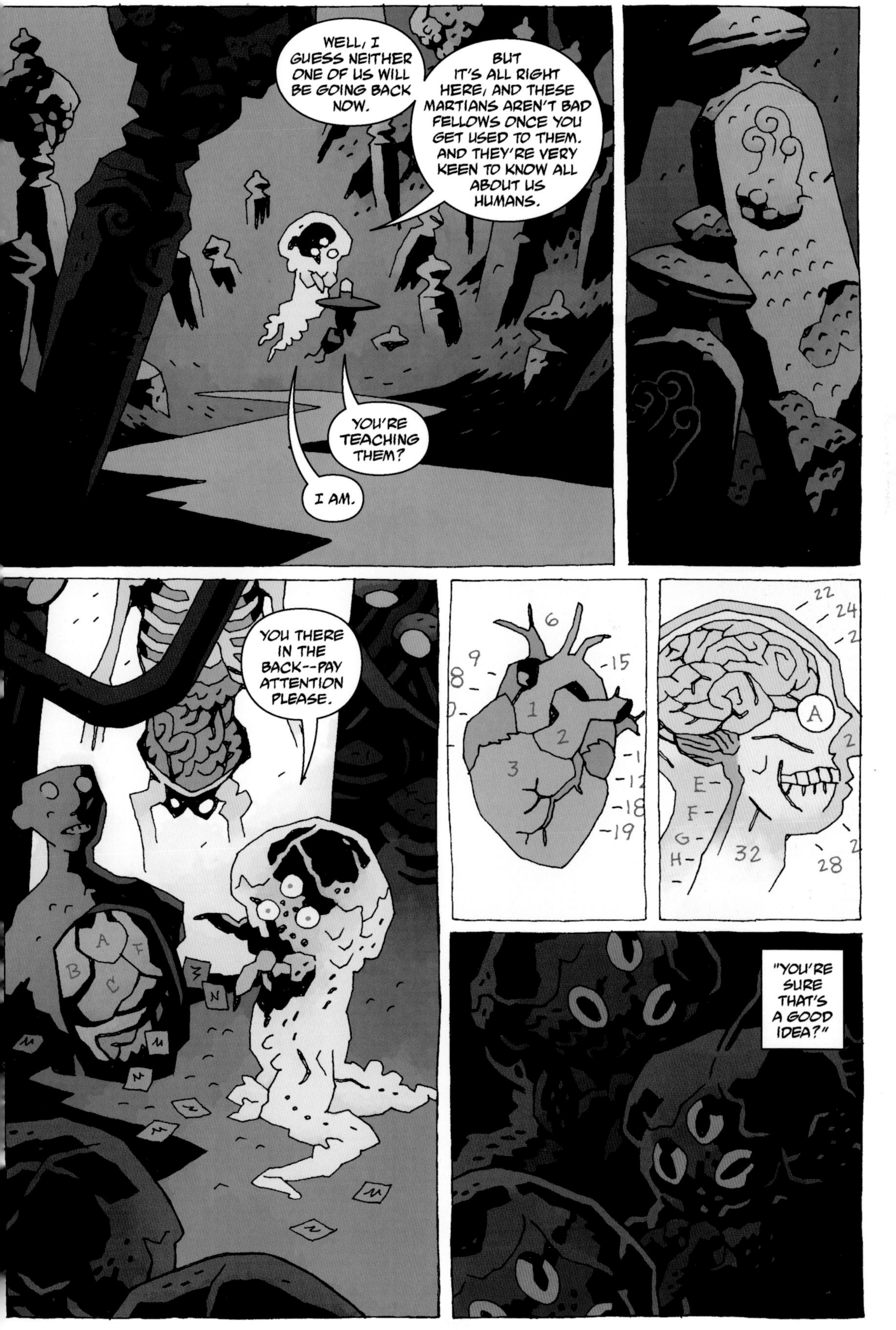

WELL, I GUESS NEITHER ONE OF US WILL BE GOING BACK NOW.
BUT IT'S ALL RIGHT HERE, AND THESE MARTIANS AREN'T BAD FELLOWS ONCE YOU GET USED TO THEM. AND THEY'RE VERY KEEN TO KNOW ALL ABOUT US HUMANS.
YOU'RE TEACHING THEM?
I AM.
YOU THERE IN THE BACK--PAY ATTENTION PLEASE.
"YOU'RE SURE THAT'S A GOOD IDEA?"

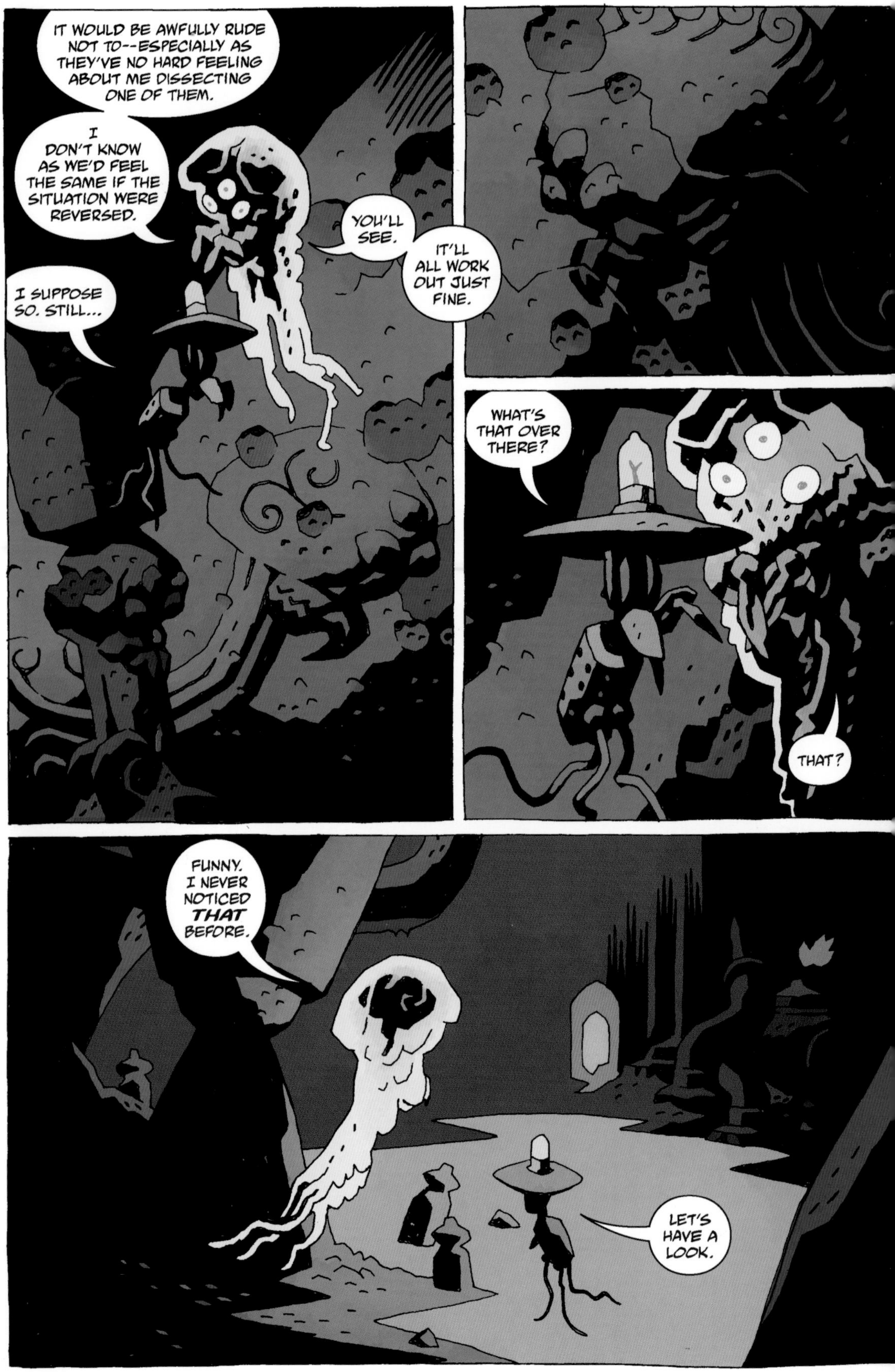
IT WOULD BE AWFULLY RUDE NOT TO--ESPECIALLY AS THEY'VE NO HARD FEELING ABOUT ME DISSECTING ONE OF THEM.
I DON'T KNOW AS WE'D FEEL THE SAME IF THE SITUATION WERE REVERSED.
YOU'LL SEE.
IT'LL ALL WORK OUT JUST FINE.
I SUPPOSE SO. STILL...
WHAT'S THAT OVER THERE?
THAT?
FUNNY. I NEVER NOTICED THAT BEFORE.
LET'S HAVE A LOOK.

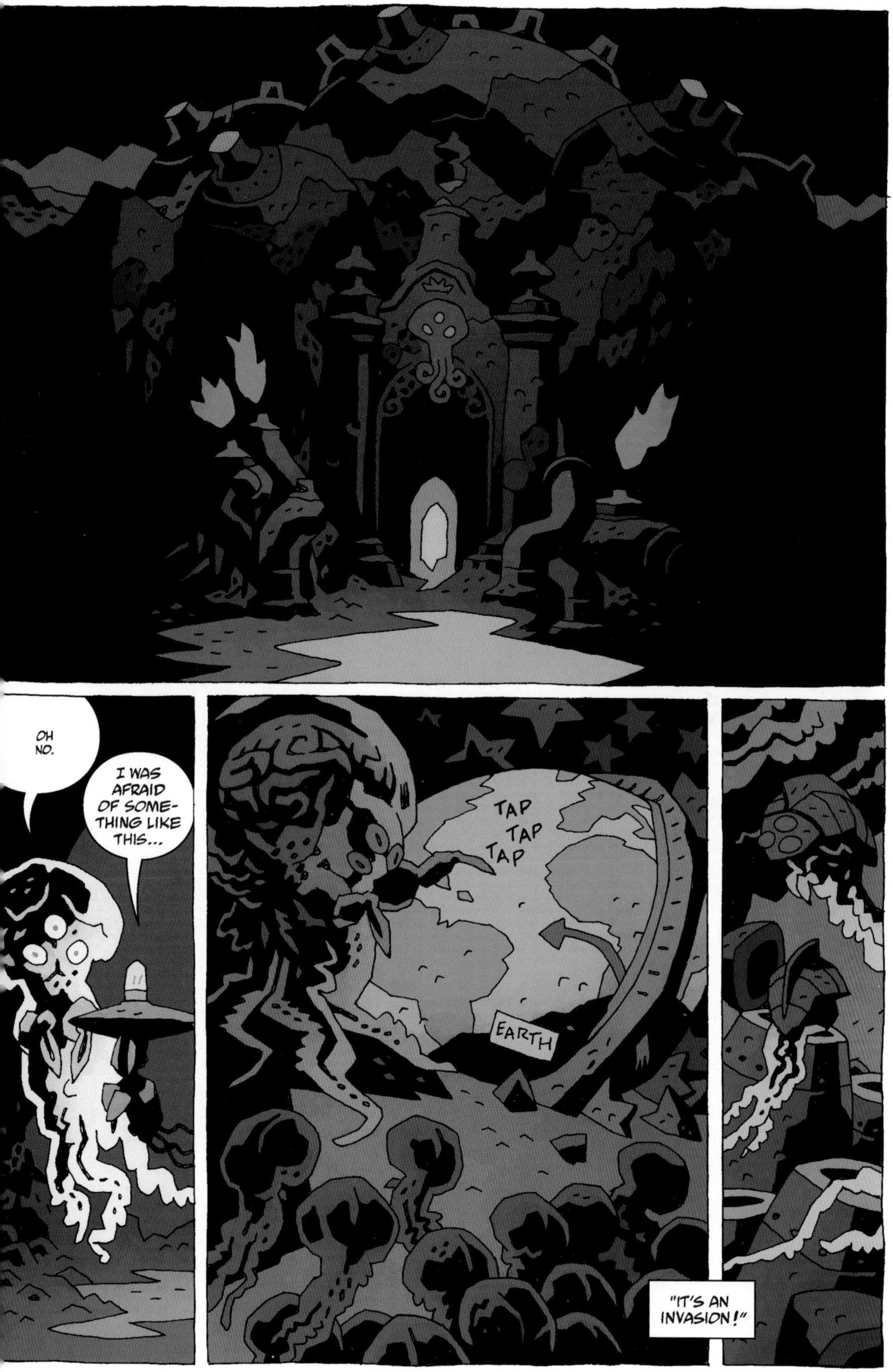

OH NO.
I WAS AFRAID OF SOME-THING LIKE THIS...
TAP TAP TAP
EARTH
"IT'S AN INVASION!"

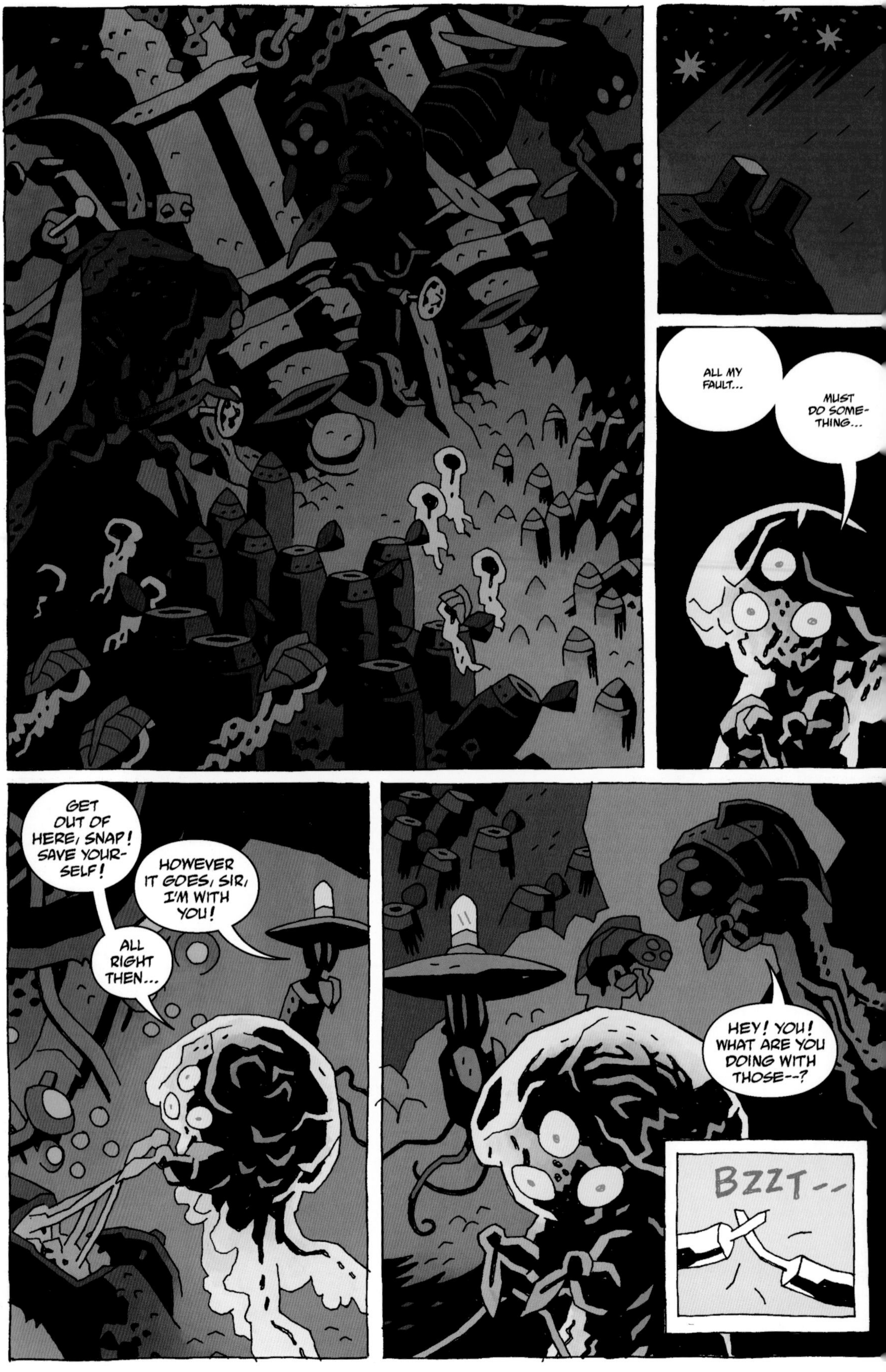

ALL MY FAULT...
MUST DO SOME-THING...
GET OUT OF HERE, SNAP! SAVE YOUR-SELF!
HOWEVER IT GOES, SIR, I'M WITH YOU!
ALL RIGHT THEN...
HEY! YOU! WHAT ARE YOU DOING WITH THOSE--?
BZZT--

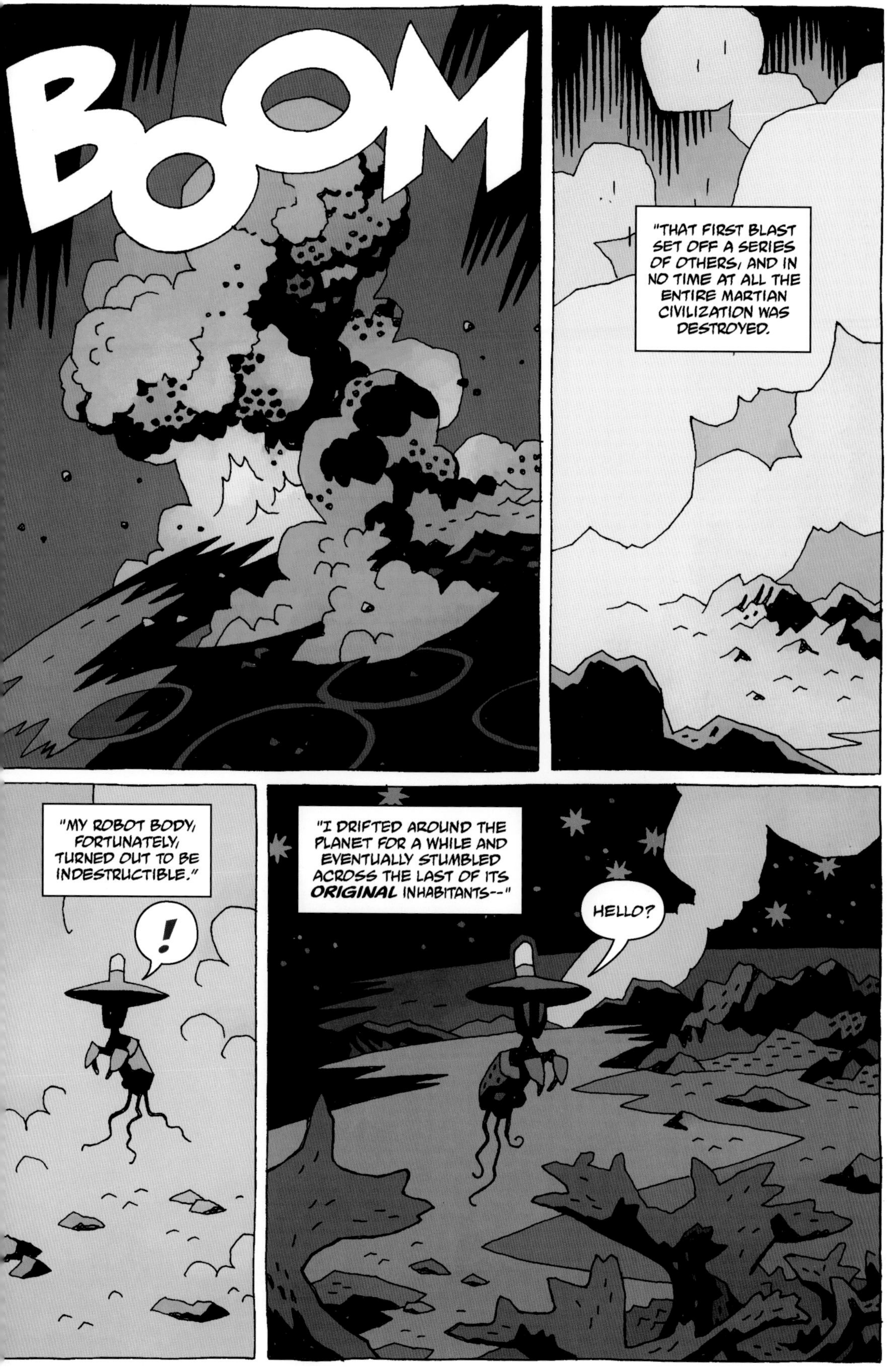
BOOM
"THAT FIRST BLAST SET OFF A SERIES OF OTHERS, AND IN NO TIME AT ALL THE ENTIRE MARTIAN CIVILIZATION WAS DESTROYED.
"MY ROBOT BODY, FORTUNATELY, TURNED OUT TO BE INDESTRUCTIBLE."
!
"I DRIFTED AROUND THE PLANET FOR A WHILE AND EVENTUALLY STUMBLED ACROSS THE LAST OF ITS ORIGINAL INHABITANTS--"
HELLO?

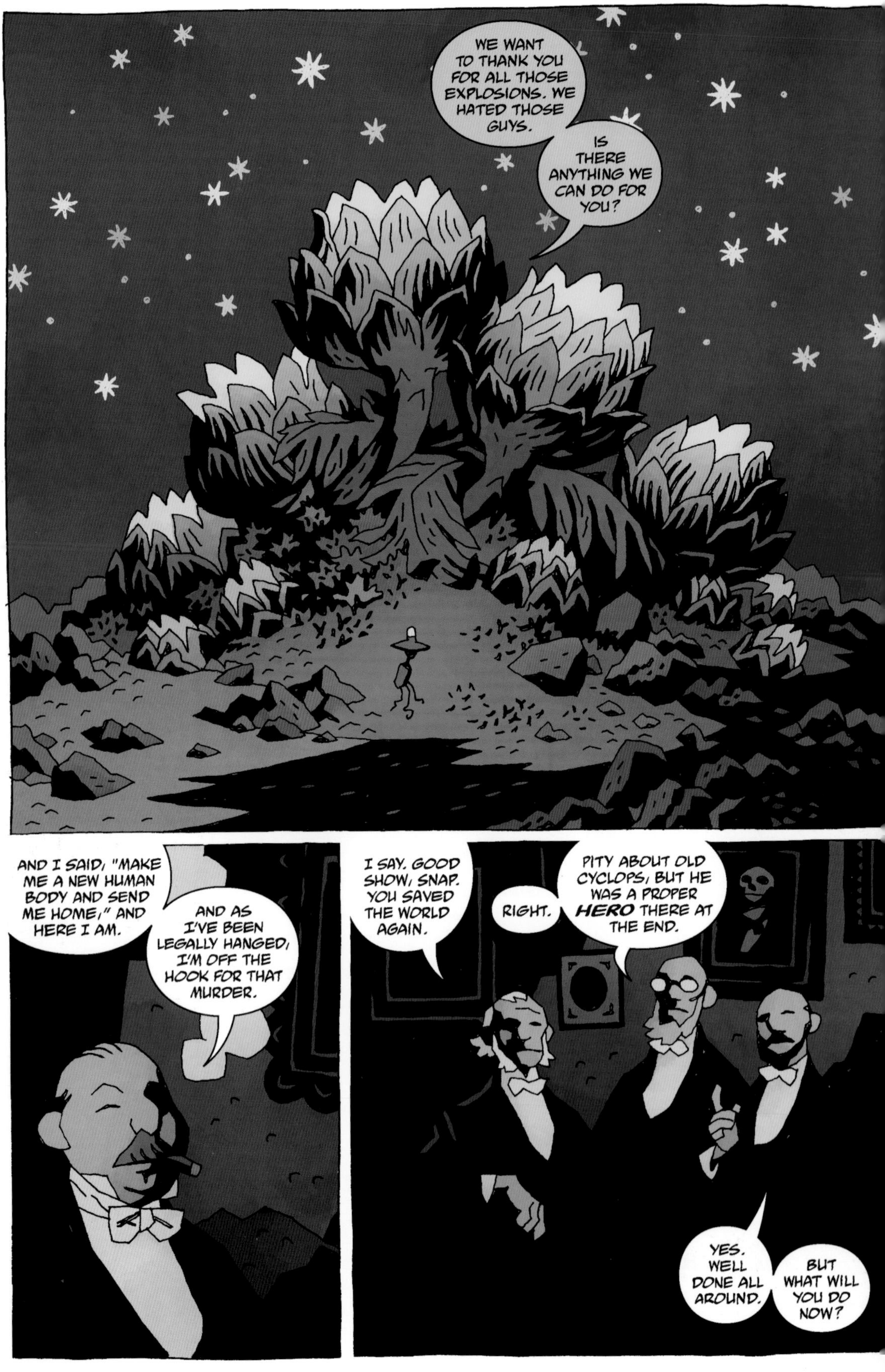
WE WANT TO THANK YOU FOR ALL THOSE EXPLOSIONS. WE HATED THOSE GUYS.
IS THERE ANYTHING WE CAN DO FOR YOU?
AND I SAID, "MAKE ME A NEW HUMAN BODY AND SEND ME HOME," AND HERE I AM.
AND AS I'VE BEEN LEGALLY HANGED, I'M OFF THE HOOK FOR THAT MURDER.
I SAY. GOOD SHOW, SNAP. YOU SAVED THE WORLD AGAIN.
RIGHT.
PITY ABOUT OLD CYCLOPS, BUT HE WAS A PROPER **HERO** THERE AT THE END.
YES. WELL DONE ALL AROUND.
BUT WHAT WILL YOU DO NOW?

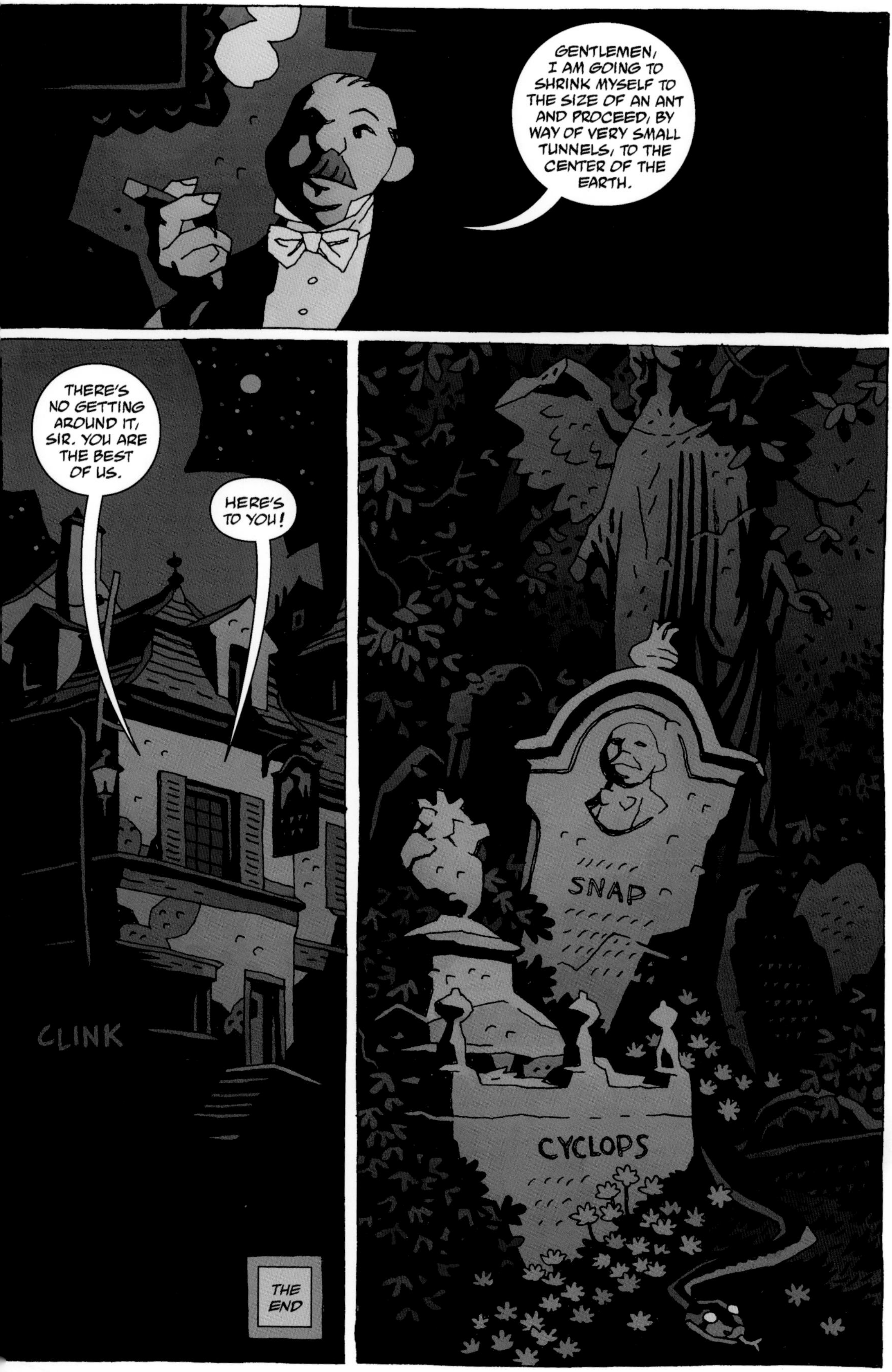
GENTLEMEN, I AM GOING TO SHRINK MYSELF TO THE SIZE OF AN ANT AND PROCEED, BY WAY OF VERY SMALL TUNNELS, TO THE CENTER OF THE EARTH.
THERE'S NO GETTING AROUND IT, SIR. YOU ARE THE BEST OF US.
HERE'S TO YOU!
CLINK
THE END
SNAP
CYCLOPS

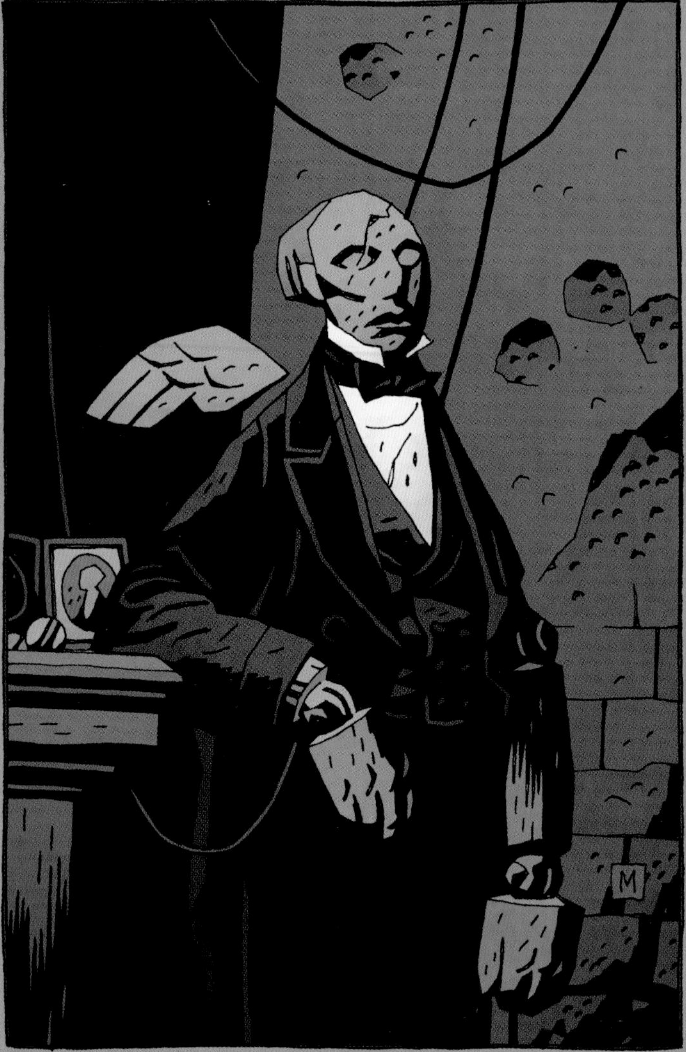

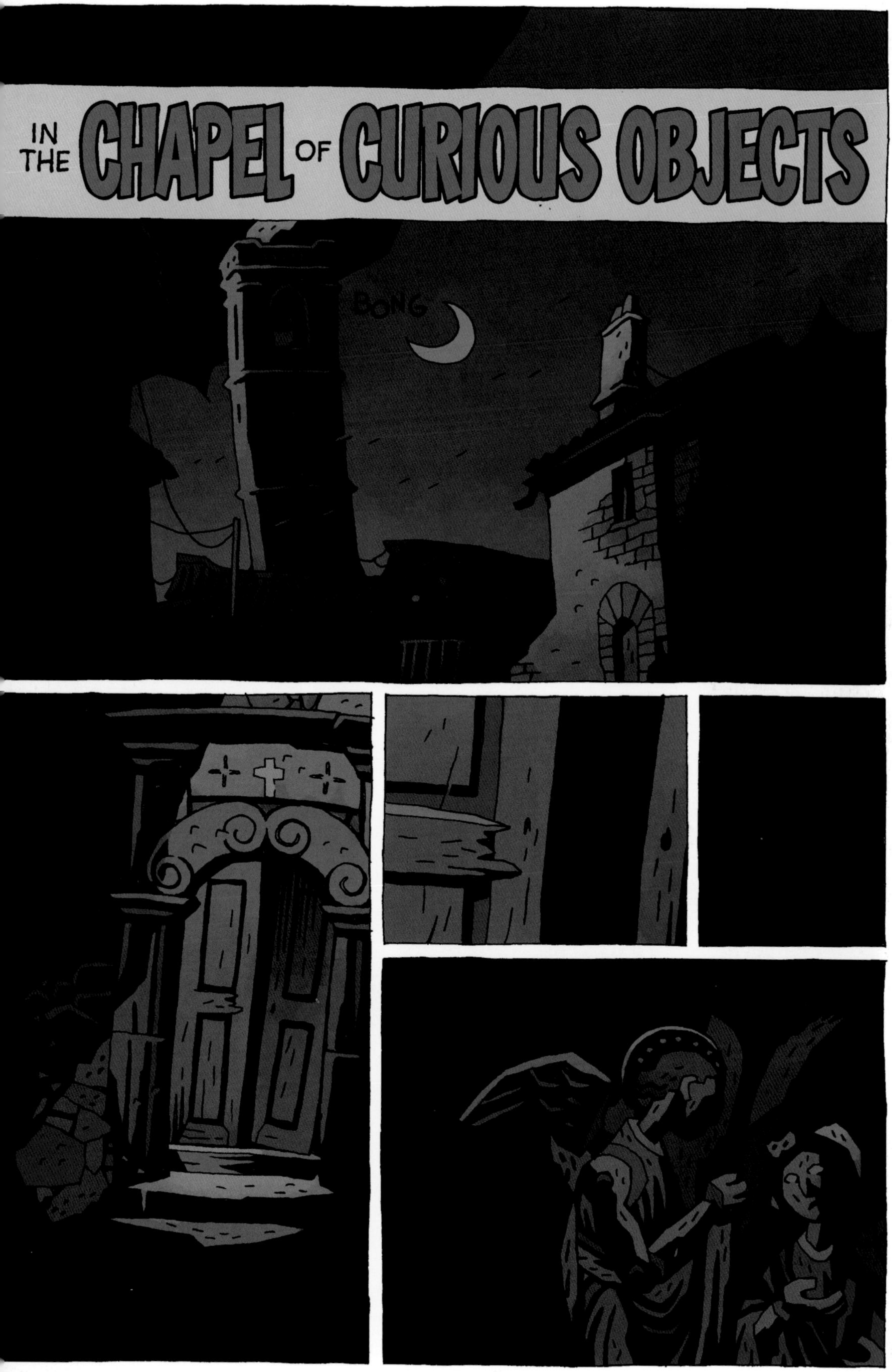
IN THE CHAPEL OF CURIOUS OBJECTS
BONG

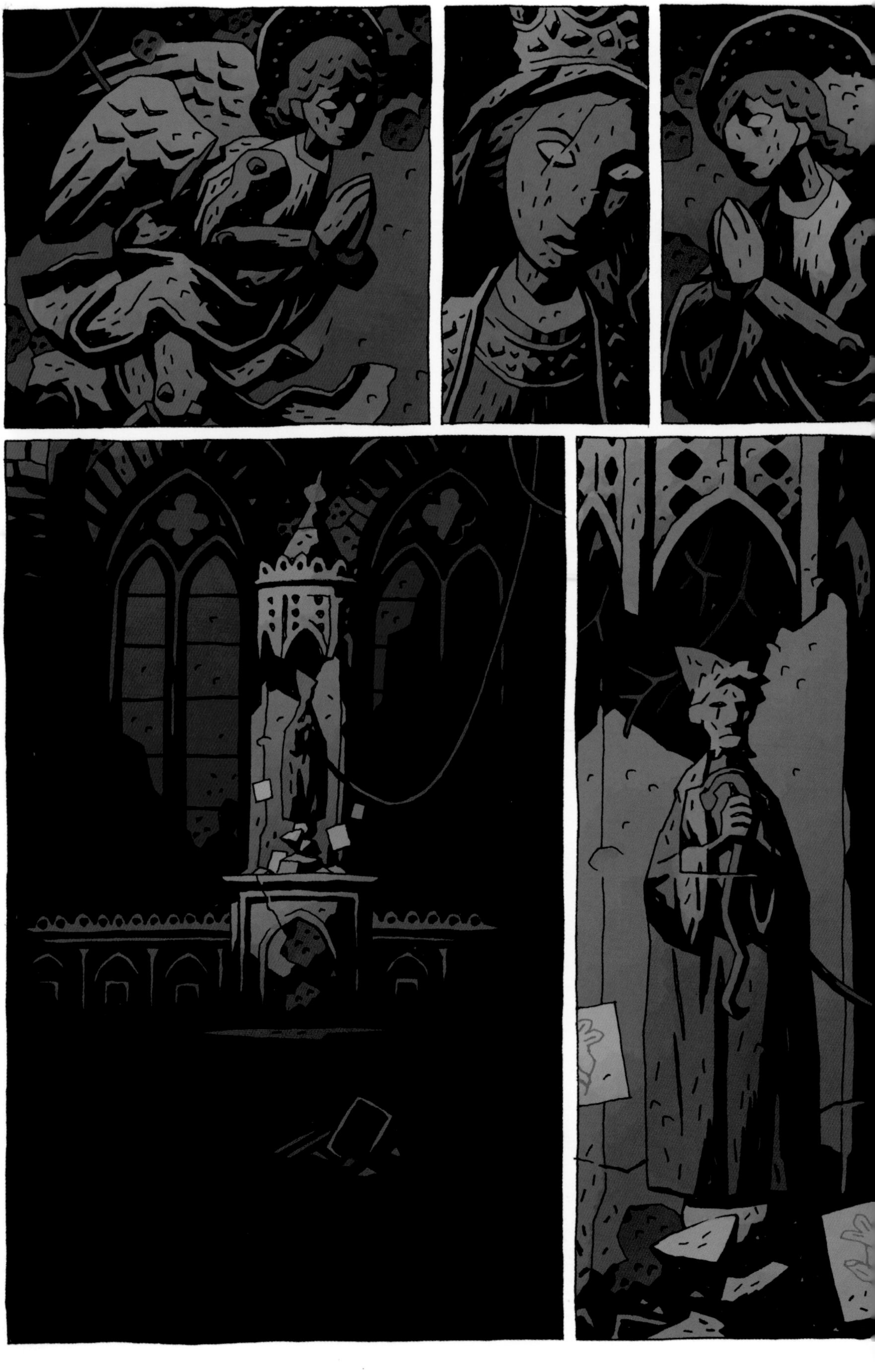

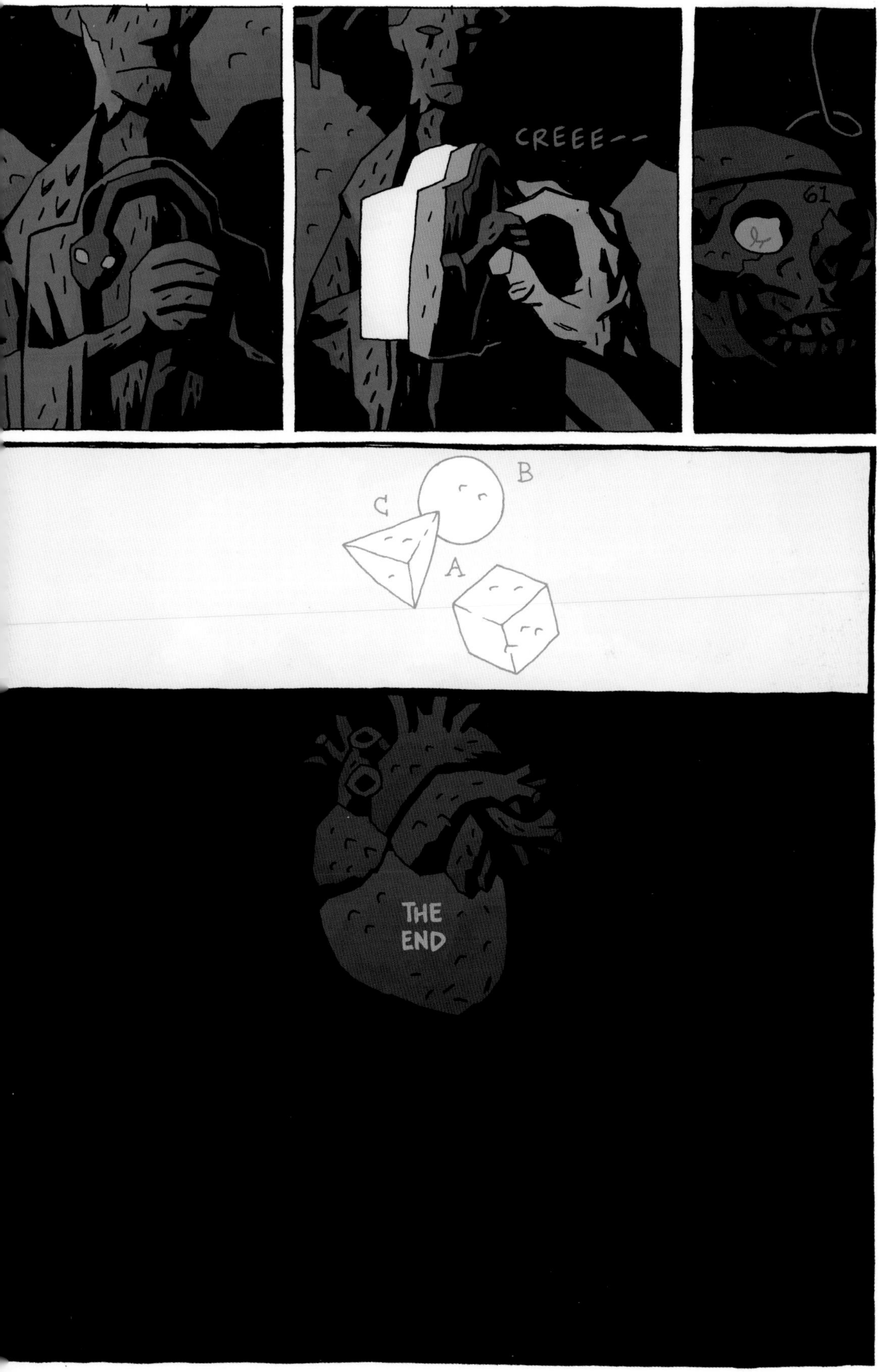
CREEE--
61
B
C
A
THE END

STORY NOTES

THE AMAZING SCREW-ON HEAD started out as an idea for a toy. It wasn't a serious idea, just a thought—a robot head, threaded like a light bulb, that you could screw into different robot bodies. I like that. I still want that toy. But I'm not a toy designer so I turned the thing into a comic. At first it was going to be something very fun and modern, the kind of thing Nickelodeon makes cartoons out of, but as I started getting serious about drawing it, it started to slide into the kind of stuff I really like to draw—low-tech machines, statues, rooftops, and old, dusty Victorians. And if there was going to be a president in it, he was going to have to be Lincoln. In the end (and the whole thing went pretty fast), I created a comic that was pretty much just for me. I didn't expect anyone else to care about it, so I was pretty surprised when right away people started telling me it was the best thing I'd ever done. I like when *that* happens. It was published as a one-issue comic in 2002 and won the 2003 Eisner Award for Best Humor Publication.

THE MAGICIAN AND THE SNAKE: One day an editor at Dark Horse called and asked me to do a story for an anthology she was putting together—she only asked that it not be a Hellboy story. I said sure, but had no idea what I was going to do. A day or two later (it might have been the same day, but that seems a little too good to be true), I picked up my daughter (then age seven) from school. On the walk home, she told me about a picture she had drawn that day—a snake on a rooftop "being furious" with some floating objects. What? She went on to tell me the story behind the picture, and I remember thinking, "I'm not quite sure what this is, but it's better than anything I'm going to come up with." I drew the story pretty fast and I only recall one snag—I wanted the magician to be a Victorian stage magician, but my daughter (being seven) insisted on the pointed hat. I think she was right. The story appeared in the book *Happy Endings* (I swear I didn't know that was the title when I did the story) in 2002 and won the 2003 Eisner Award for Best Short Story. That was a good year.

ABU GUNG AND THE BEANSTALK was originally done back in 1998 for the Dark Horse anthology *Scatterbrain*. I always liked the story (and most of the dialogue) but was never happy with the way it was drawn. For this book I've completely redrawn it and expanded it from five pages to nine—mostly so I could work in that exciting bean-sprouting sequence.

THE WITCH AND HER SOUL sprang into my head fully formed one day, complete with the names Hankel and Manx, which is a good thing because I could never have made up those names—though I suppose I did.

Names are tough. The only real trouble I had with THE PRISONER OF MARS was coming up with a name for the murdered professor. For a while his name was going to be Mister Kaleidoscope, but fortunately I came to my senses. Both "The Witch and Her Soul" and "The Prisoner of Mars" were done specifically for this book.

IN THE CHAPEL OF CURIOUS OBJECTS isn't a story at all. It just felt like it was the thing needed to finish the book, to maybe tie the whole thing together in a way that can't quite be explained—like a little hat for an oddly shaped head. And that's about all there is to say about that.

THE END

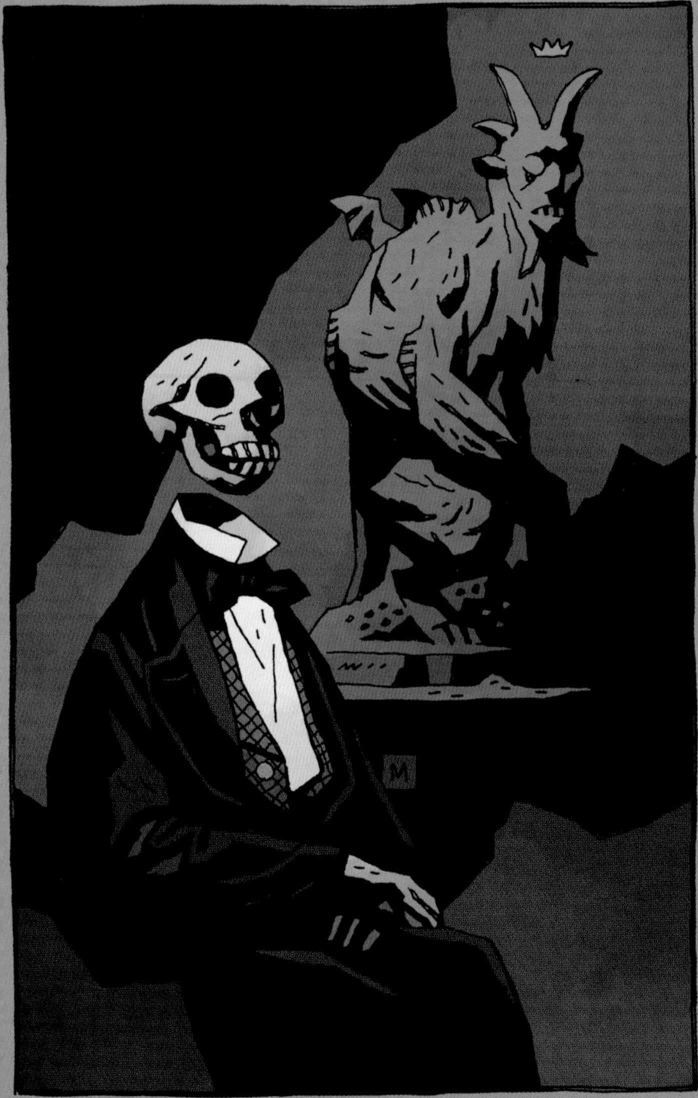

SKETCHBOOK

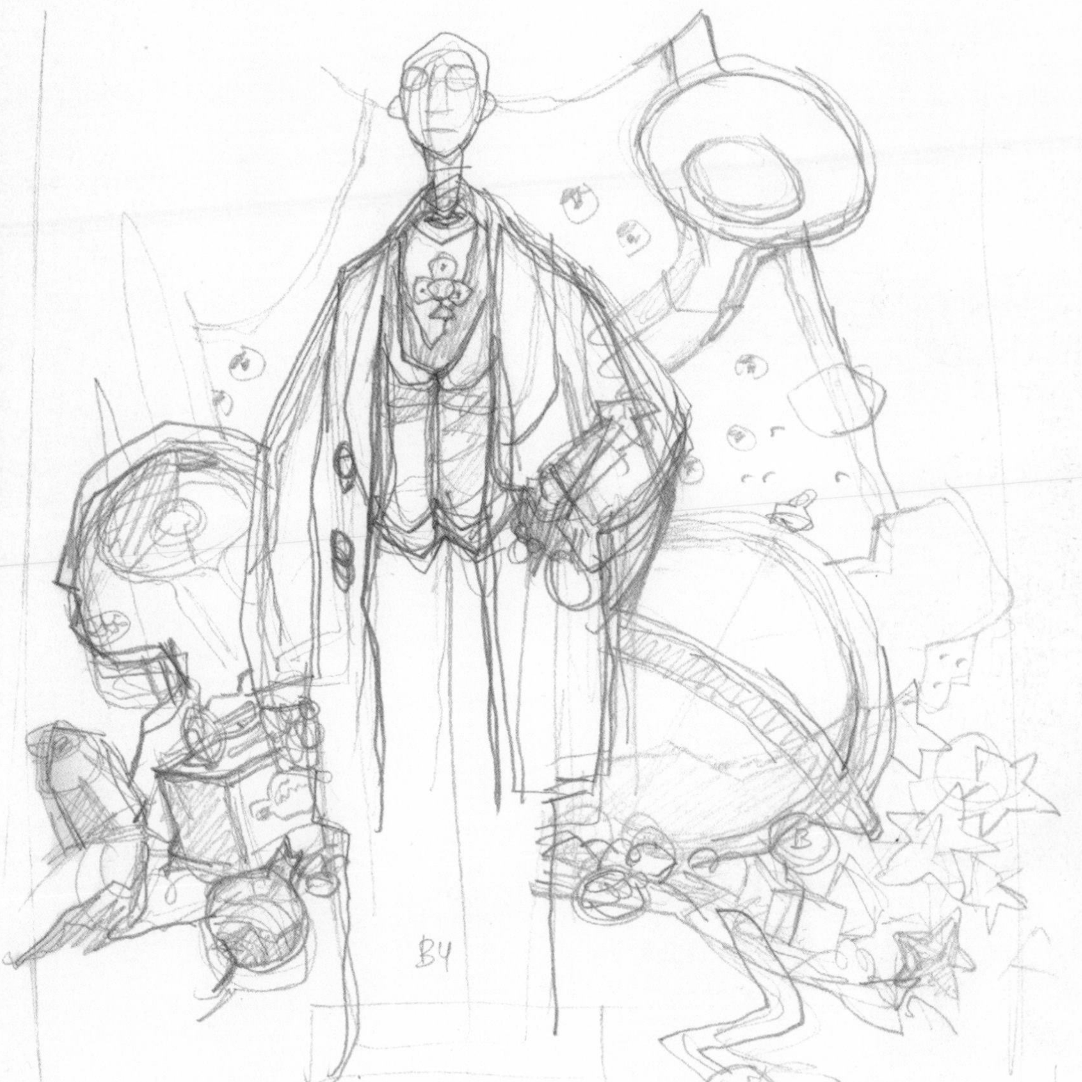

B4

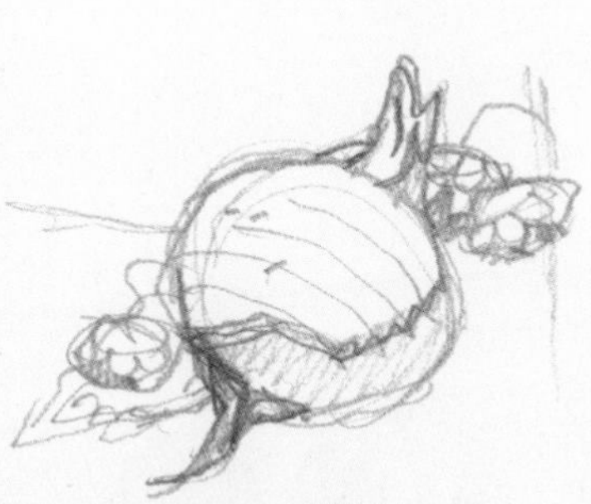

Rough for the cover of this book. Actually this was my second version of the cover. I finished the first version (now page 2 of this book) and was very happy with it, but just felt that something more formal might suit the title better.

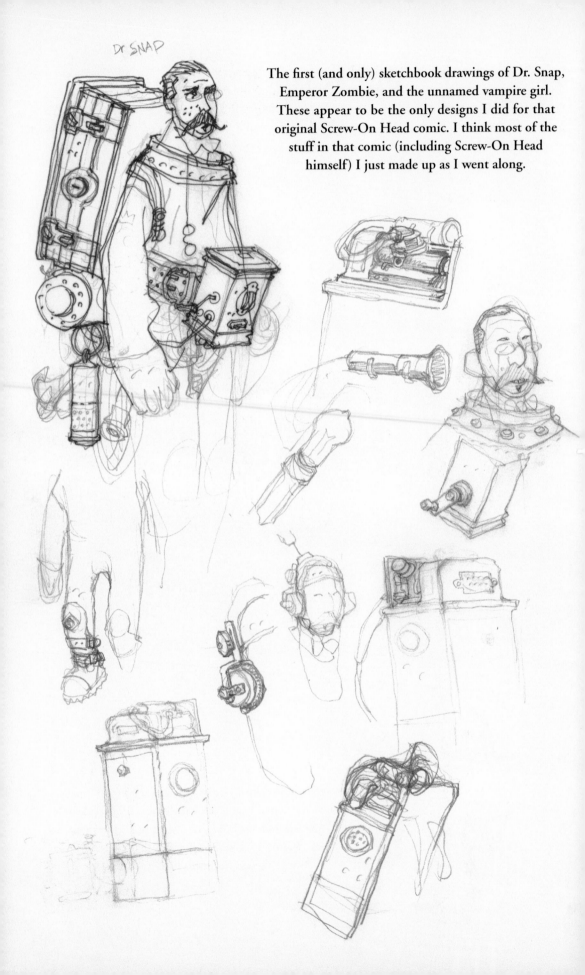

Dr SNAP

The first (and only) sketchbook drawings of Dr. Snap,
Emperor Zombie, and the unnamed vampire girl.
These appear to be the only designs I did for that
original Screw-On Head comic. I think most of the
stuff in that comic (including Screw-On Head
himself) I just made up as I went along.

There are no untold Screw-On Head stories. Everything I wanted to do with him I did in that one comic. That doesn't mean I don't love him—so nothing should be read into the fact that the only new drawing I did of the character for this book (other than the covers) is a drawing of him being torn to pieces by giant crabs.

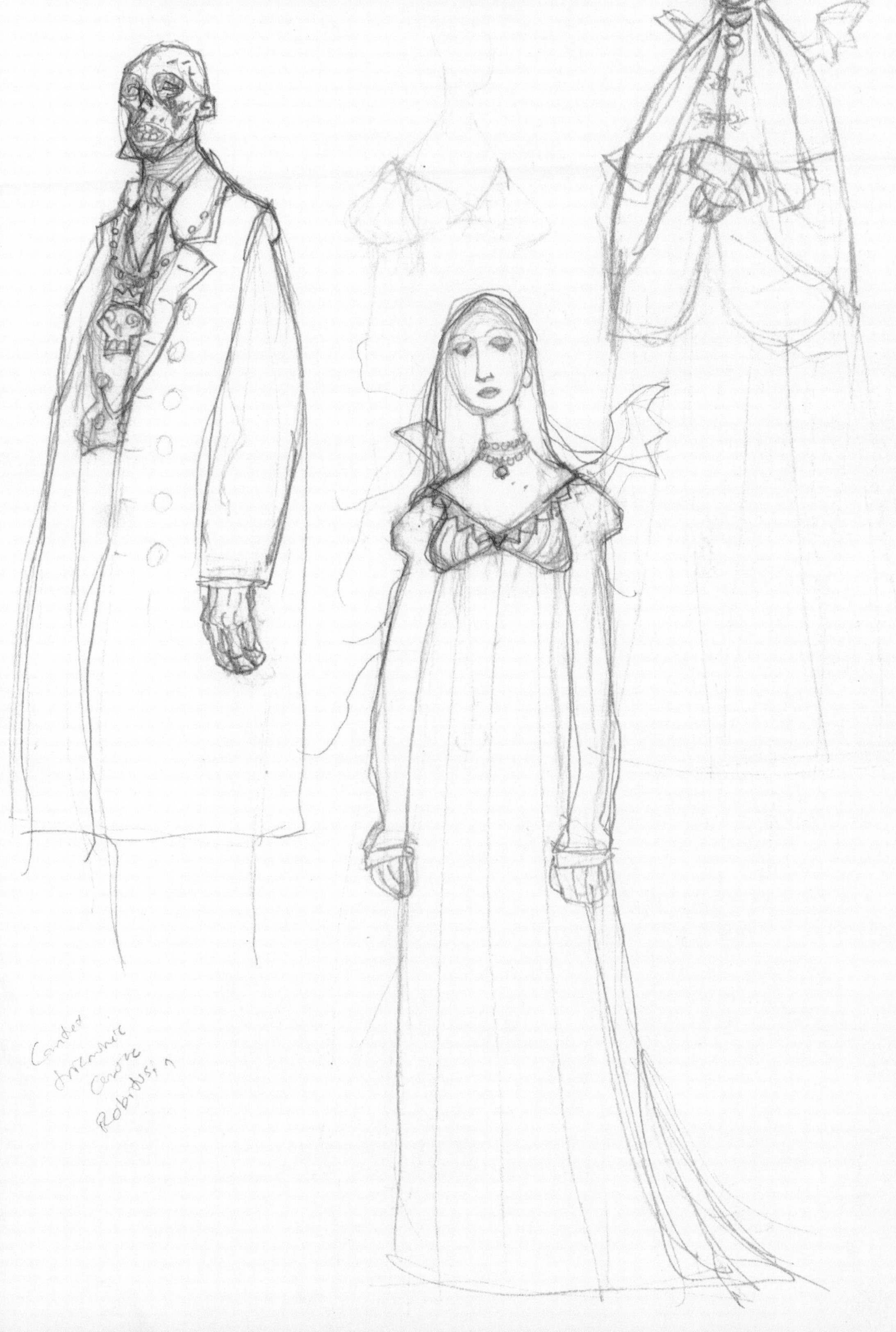

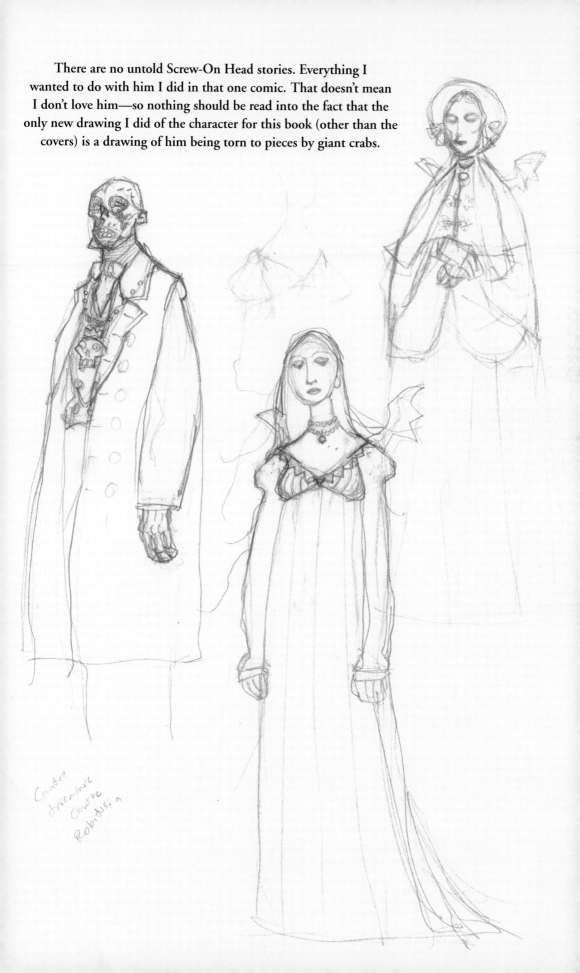

While this new version of "Abu Gung and the Beanstalk" is much better drawn than the original, most of the character designs are pretty much the same—though in the original the devil had a (badly drawn) bird instead of a bat, and he didn't have that snazzy little umbrella.

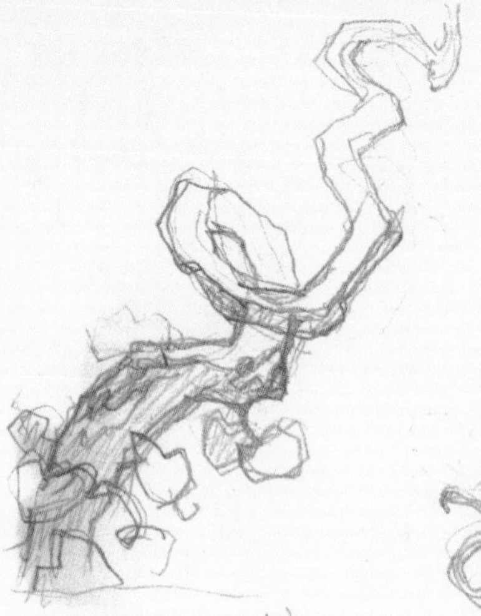

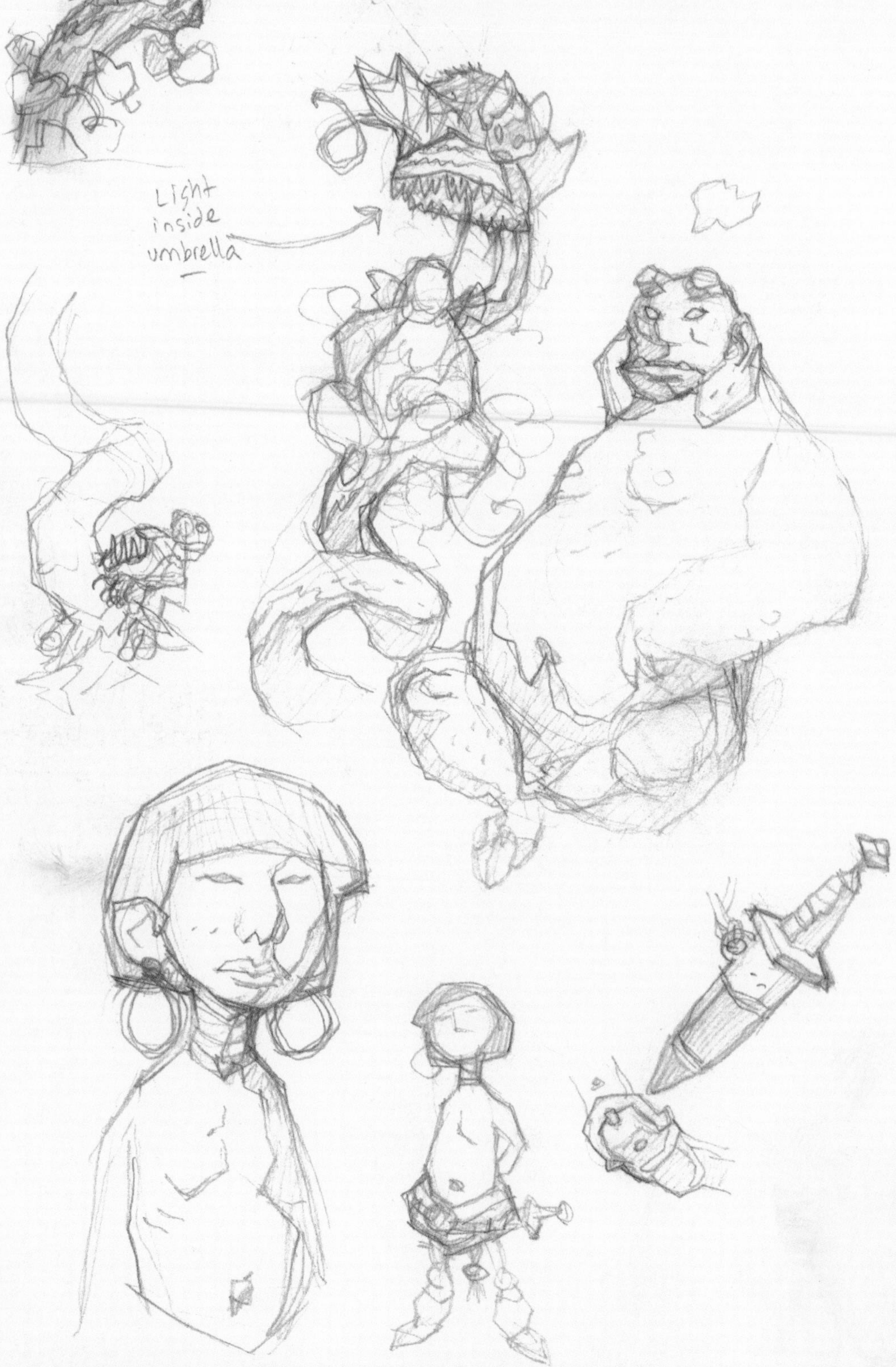
Light inside umbrella

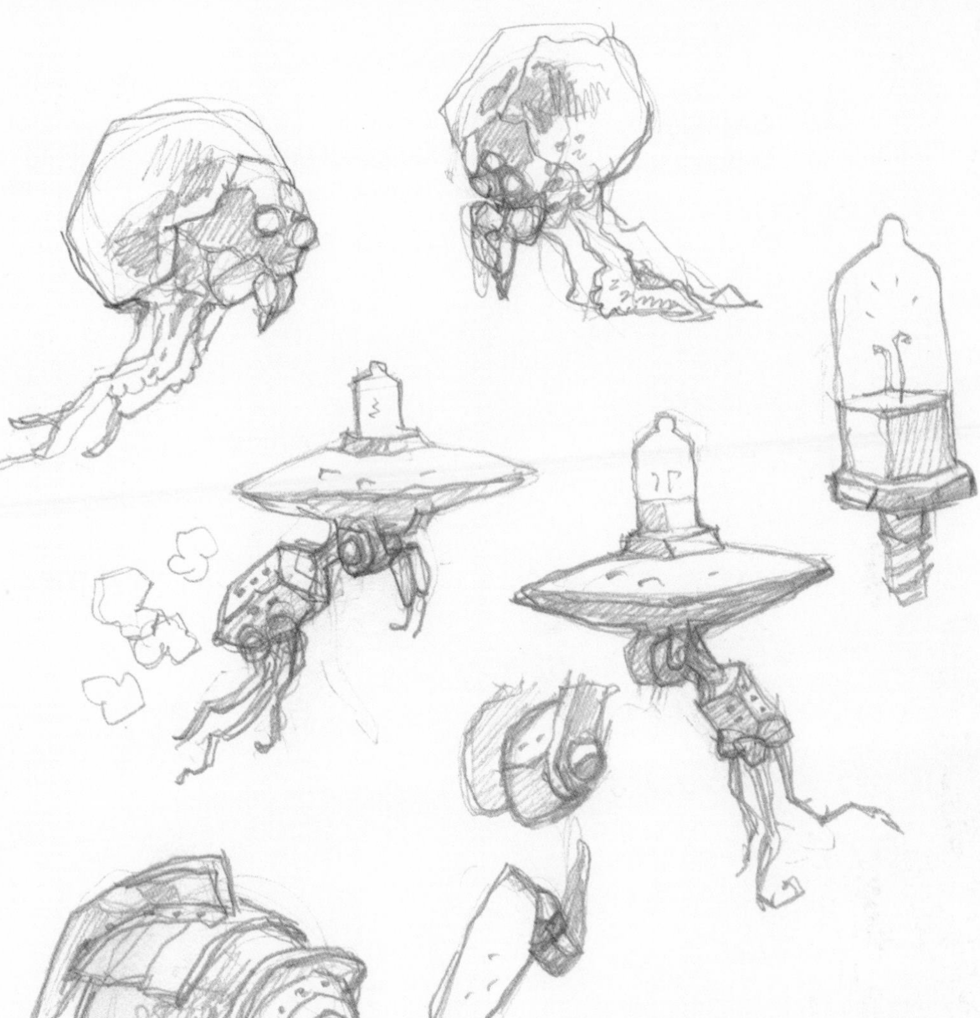
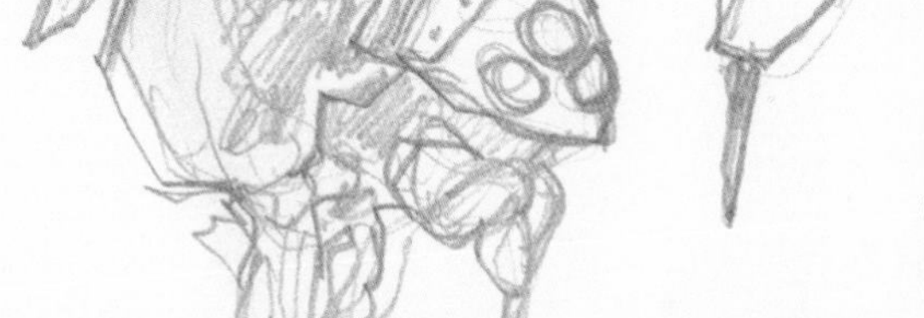

For the little robot body in "The Prisoner of Mars," I always had in mind "something like a cross between a bagpipe and an accordion," but when it came time to draw that I had no idea what it would look like—so I came up with this sputtering, flying pan instead.

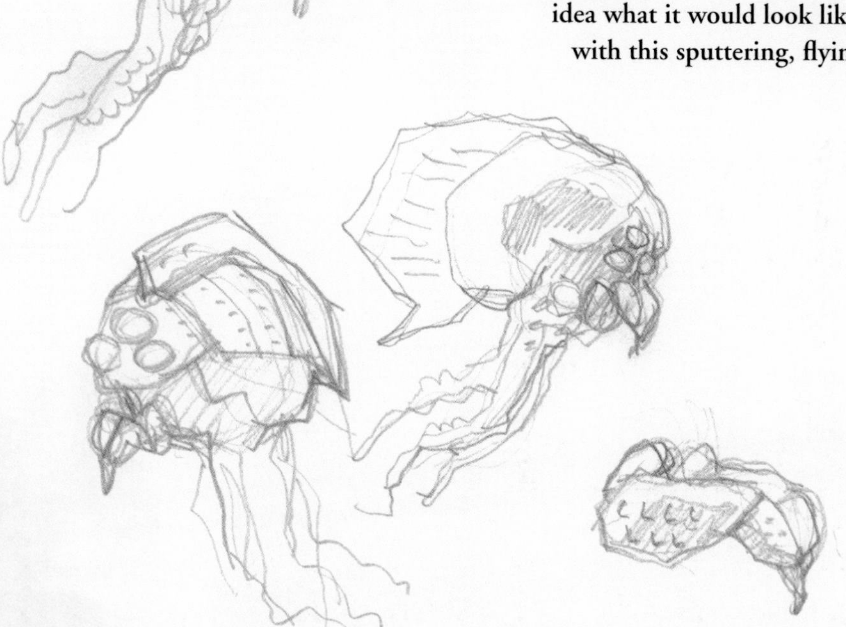

More Mars stuff.

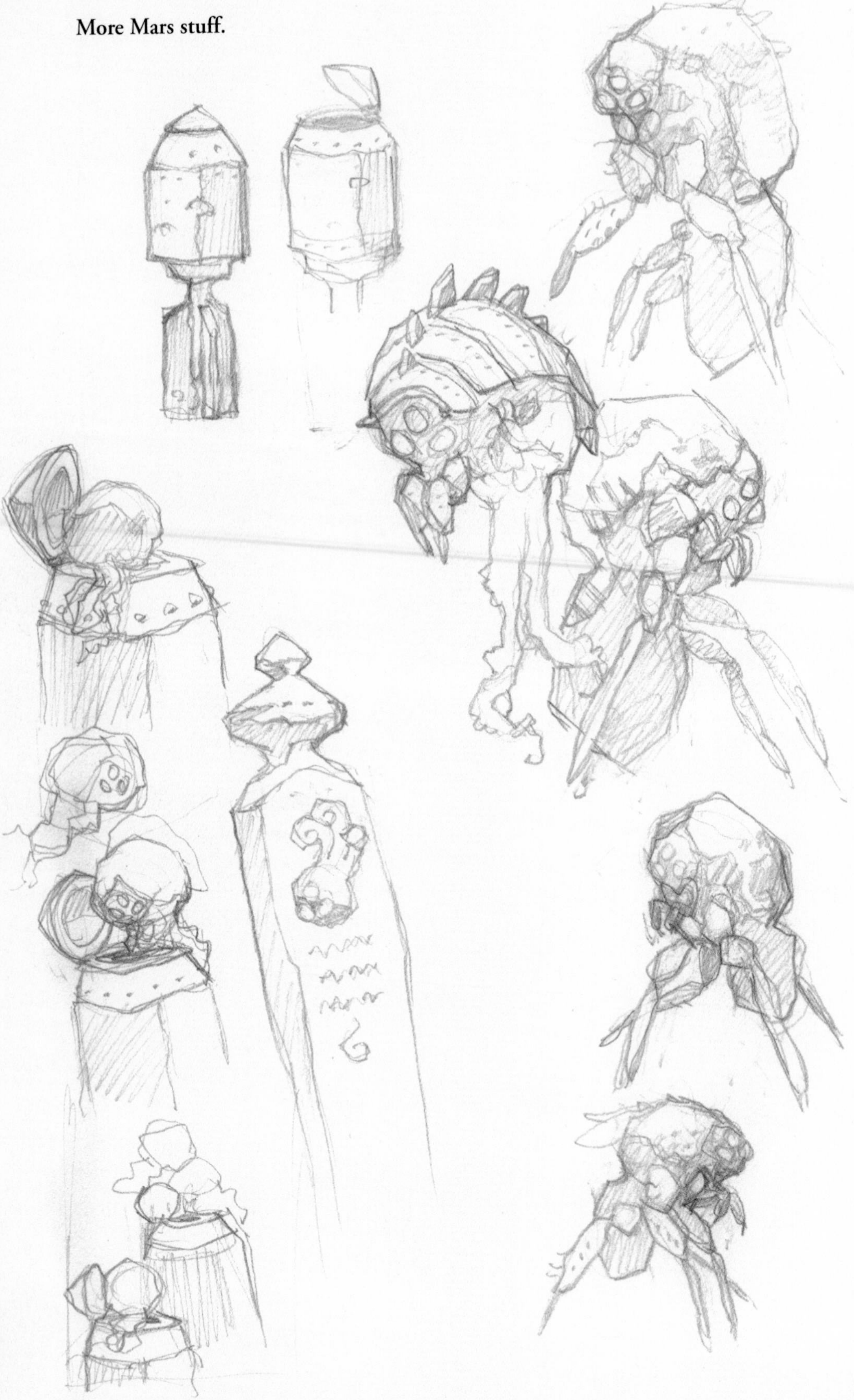

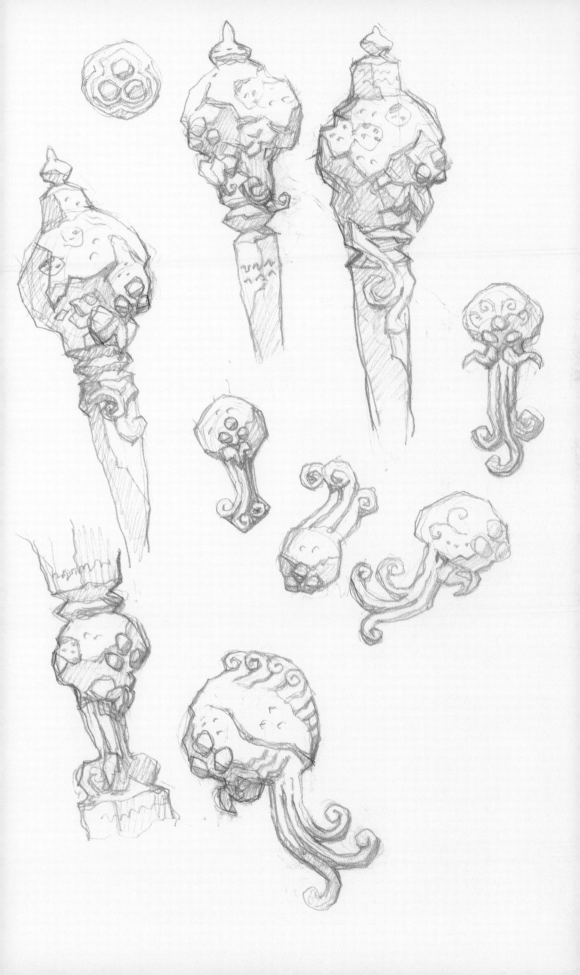

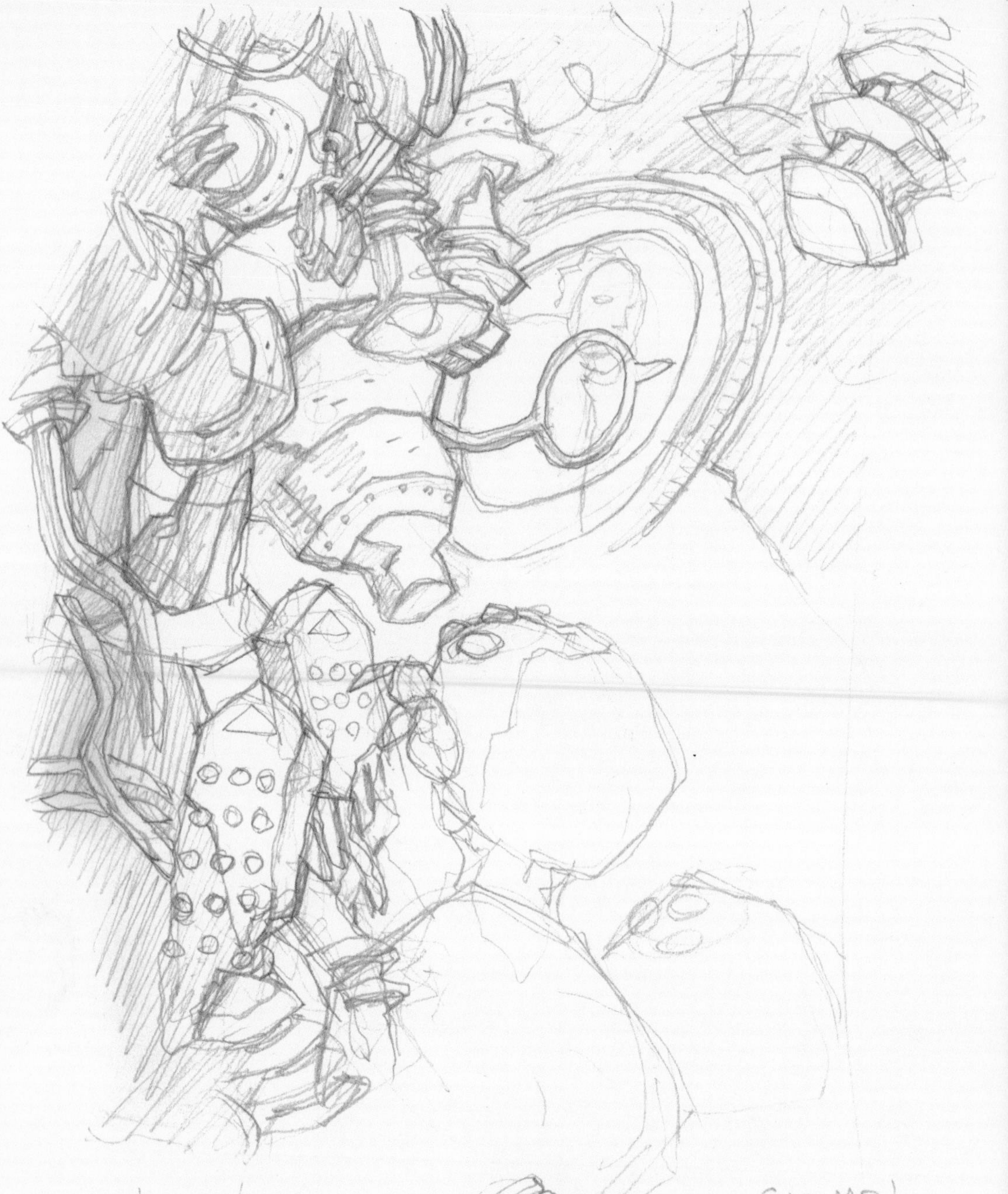

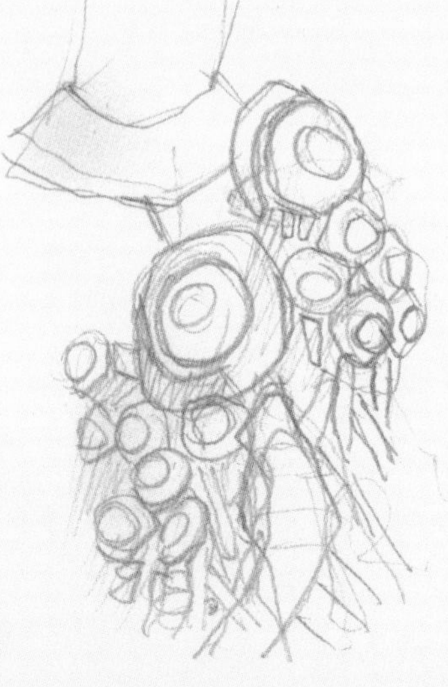

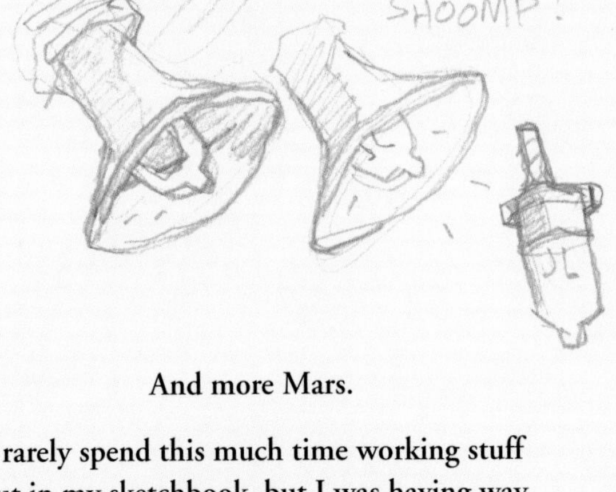
SHOOMP!

And more Mars.

I rarely spend this much time working stuff out in my sketchbook, but I was having way too much fun with these guys.

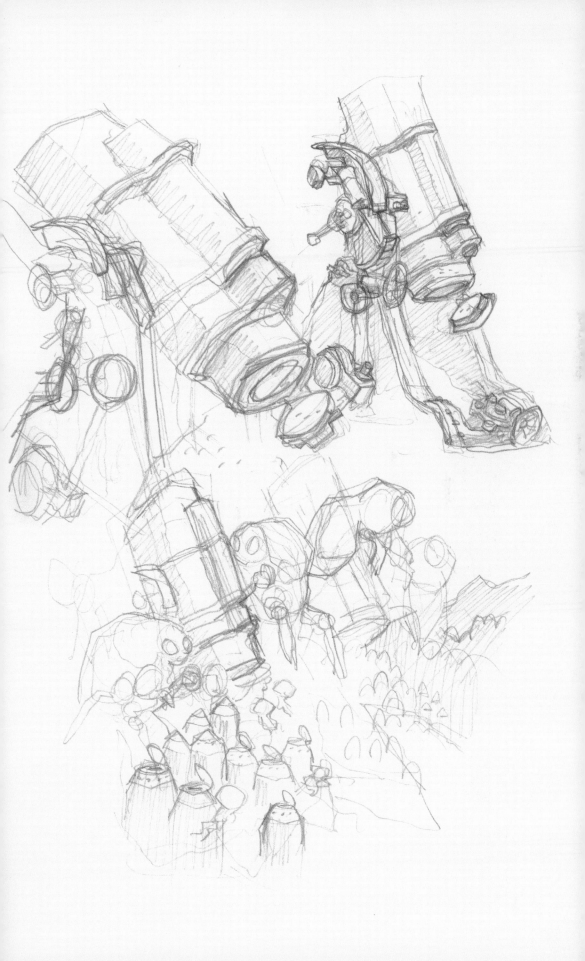

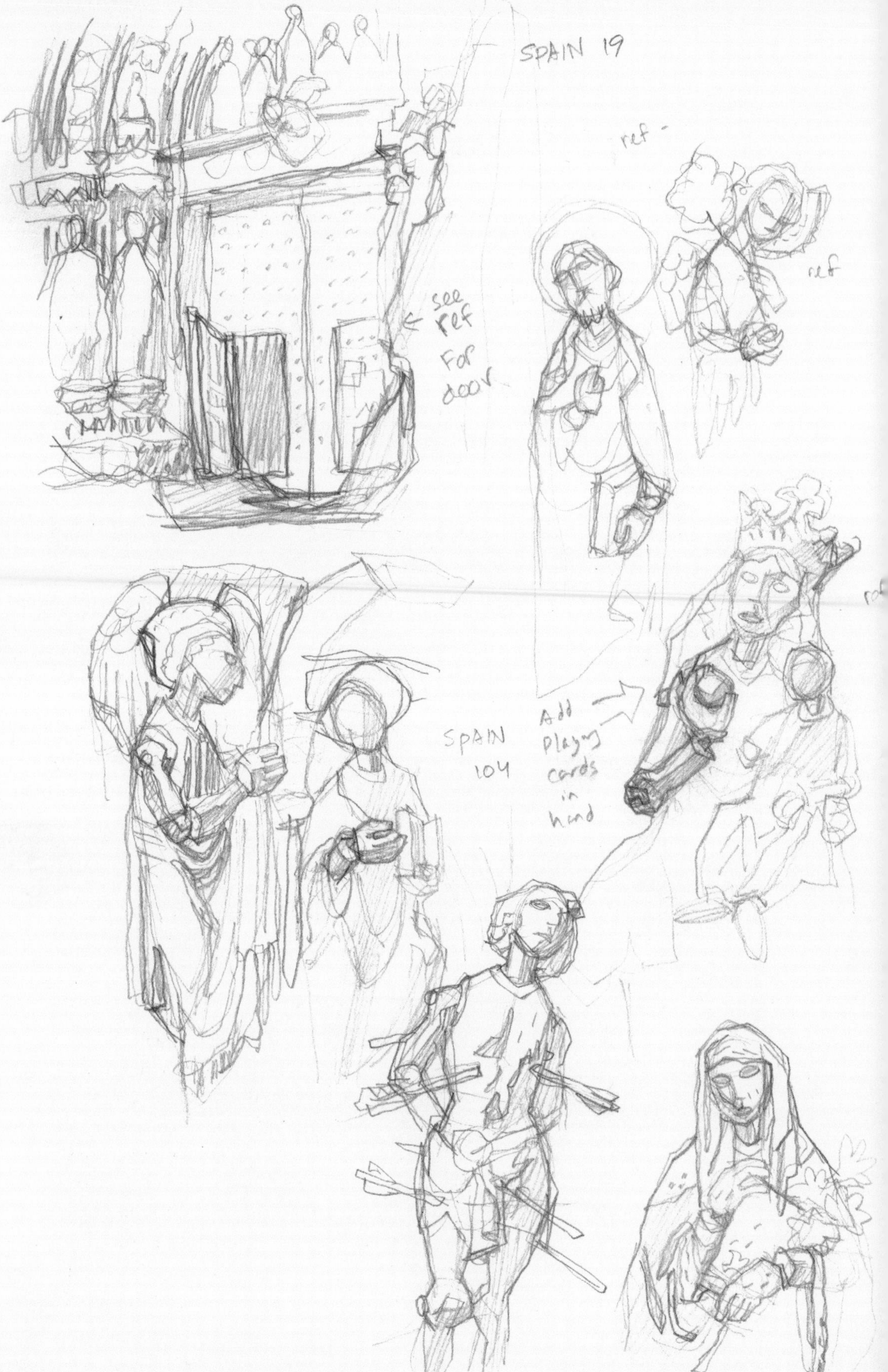
SPAIN 19
ref -
ref
see ref for door
SPAIN 104
Add playing cards in hand

An unused doorway (far left), plus puppets and more puppets.

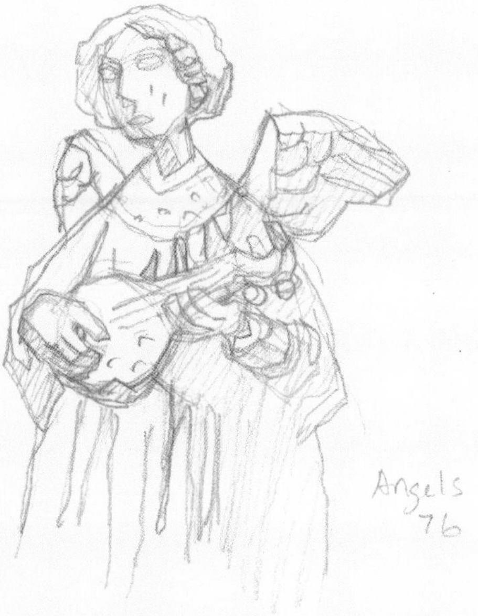
Angels
76

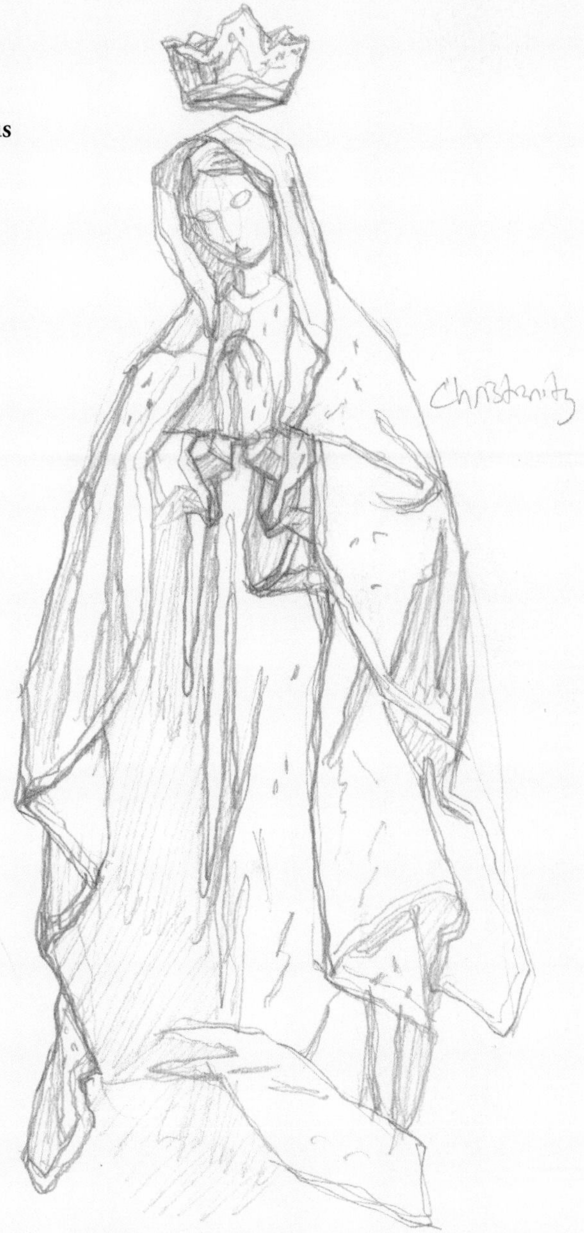
Christianity

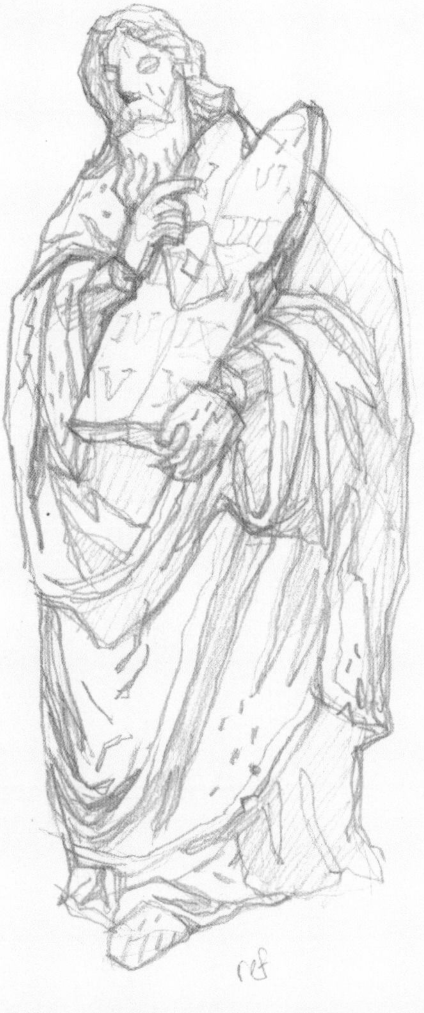
ref

These are just a few of the dozens of puppets I designed. I was still having way too much fun, and "In the Chapel of Curious Objects" was originally going to be longer, with more pages of drifting through the chapel, looking at puppets. I was never going to get tired of drawing those puppets, but in the end I was afraid the reader might get tired of looking at them. They say less is more . . . though I'm not sure if that really applies to spooky old puppets.

MIKE MIGNOLA

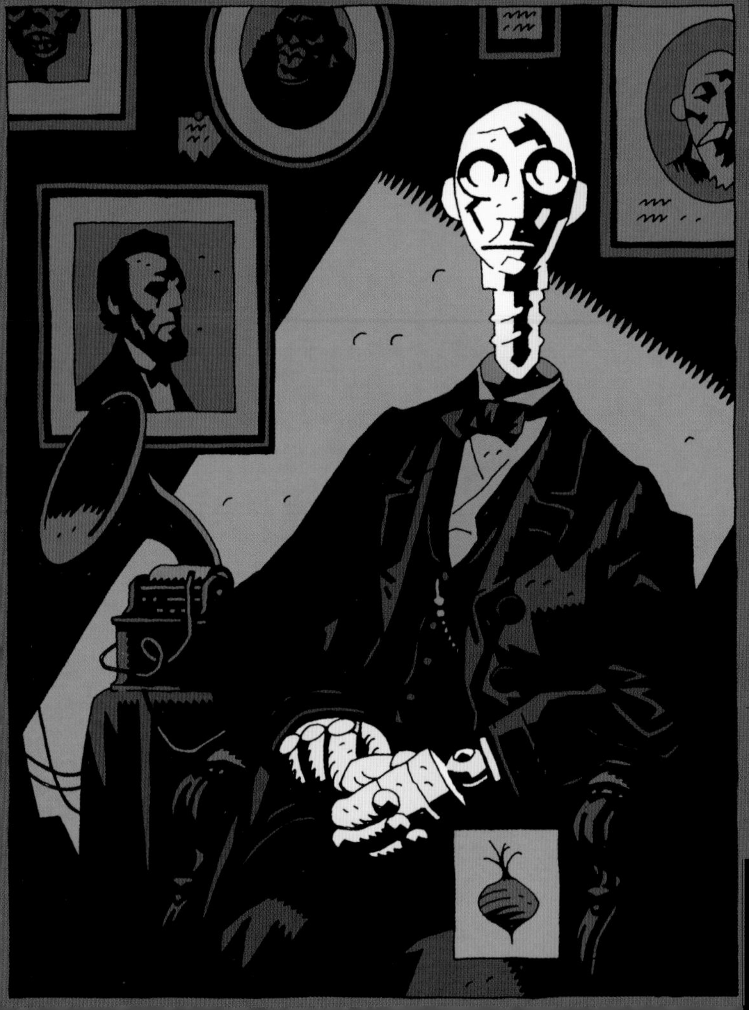

ALSO FROM DARK HORSE BOOKS

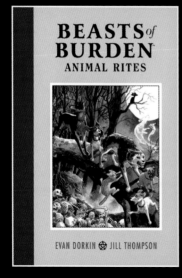

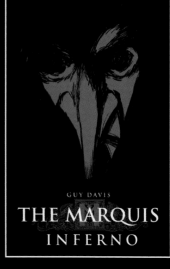

BEASTS of BURDEN
ANIMAL RITES
EVAN DORKIN JILL THOMPSON

BEASTS OF BURDEN: ANIMAL RITES

Evan Dorkin and Jill Thompson

Beneath its shiny exterior, the picturesque town of Burden Hill harbors dark and sinister secrets, and it's up to a heroic gang of dogs—and one cat—to protect the town from the evil forces at work. These are the Beasts of Burden Hill.

ISBN 978-1-59582-513-1 | $19.99

GUY DAVIS
THE MARQUIS
INFERNO

THE MARQUIS VOLUME 1: INFERNO

Guy Davis

In eighteenth-century Venisalle, faith governs life and death, the guilty hide their shame behind masks, and the souls of Hell have escaped to possess the living. One man is blessed with the clarity to recognize the demons—and the means to return them to Hell.

ISBN 978-1-59582-368-7 | $24.99

COMING IN OCTOBER FROM DARK HORSE BOOKS
EXURBIA
SCOTT ALLIE
KEVIN McGOVERN

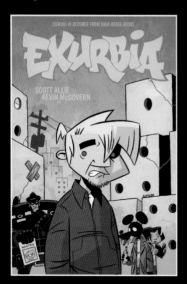

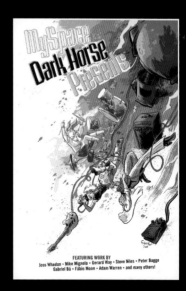

EXURBIA

Scott Allie and Kevin McGovern

Gage Wallace's day seemingly couldn't get any worse. After losing his girlfriend, he's framed for blowing up his apartment building—the latest in a string of bombings. His only hope may be a talking rat, whose drunken ramblings many take as prophecy.

ISBN 978-1-59582-339-7 | $9.99

MySpace
Dark Horse
Presents
FEATURING WORK BY
Joss Whedon • Mike Mignola • Gerard Way • Steve Niles • Peter Bagge
Gabriel Bá • Fábio Moon • Adam Warren • and many others!

MYSPACE DARK HORSE PRESENTS

MySpace Dark Horse Presents is now available in collected editions, featuring original work from such comics luminaries as Mike Mignola, Joss Whedon, Zack Whedon, Stan Sakai, Guy Davis, Gerard Way, Adam Warren, Peter Bagge, Steve Niles, and many more.

VOLUME 1
ISBN 978-1-59307-998-7 | $19.99

VOLUME 2
ISBN 978-1-59582-248-2 | $19.99

VOLUME 3
ISBN 978-1-59582-327-4 | $19.99

VOLUME 4
ISBN 978-1-59582-405-9 | $19.99

AVAILABLE AT YOUR LOCAL COMICS SHOP OR BOOKSTORE! • To find a comics shop in your area, call 1-888-266-4226.

For more information or to order direct, visit darkhorse.com or call 1-800-862-0052 Mon.–Fri. 9 AM to 5 PM Pacific Time.

DARK HORSE BOOKS®
darkhorse.com

HELLBOY

by MIKE MIGNOLA

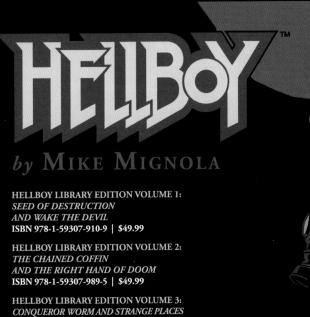

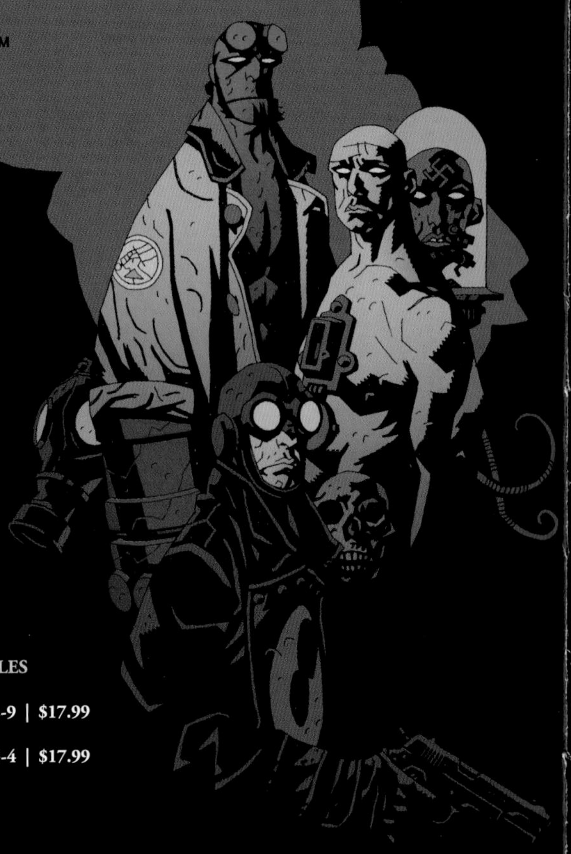

HELLBOY LIBRARY EDITION VOLUME 1:
SEED OF DESTRUCTION
AND WAKE THE DEVIL
ISBN 978-1-59307-910-9 | $49.99

HELLBOY LIBRARY EDITION VOLUME 2:
THE CHAINED COFFIN
AND THE RIGHT HAND OF DOOM
ISBN 978-1-59307-989-5 | $49.99

HELLBOY LIBRARY EDITION VOLUME 3:
CONQUEROR WORM AND STRANGE PLACES
ISBN 978-1-59582-352-6 | $49.99

✠

SEED OF DESTRUCTION
With John Byrne
ISBN 978-1-59307-094-6 | $17.99

WAKE THE DEVIL
ISBN 978-1-59307-095-3 | $17.99

THE CHAINED COFFIN AND OTHERS
ISBN 978-1-59307-091-5 | $17.99

THE RIGHT HAND OF DOOM
ISBN 978-1-59307-093-9 | $17.99

CONQUEROR WORM
ISBN 978-1-59307-092-2 | $17.99

THE TROLL WITCH AND OTHERS
ISBN 978-1-59307-860-7 | $17.99

DARKNESS CALLS
With Duncan Fegredo
ISBN 978-1-59307-896-6 | $19.99

THE WILD HUNT
With Duncan Fegredo
ISBN 978-1-59582-352-6 | $19.99

THE CROOKED MAN AND OTHERS
With Richard Corben
ISBN 978-1-59582-477-6 | $17.99

THE ART OF HELLBOY
ISBN 978-1-59307-089-2 | $29.99

HELLBOY II: THE ART OF THE MOVIE
ISBN 978-1-59307-964-2 | $24.99

HELLBOY: THE COMPANION
ISBN 978-1-59307-655-9 | $14.99

To find a comics shop in your area,
call 1-888-266-4226
For more information or to order direct:
• On the web: darkhorse.com
• E-mail: mailorder@darkhorse.com
• Phone: 1-800-862-0052
Mon.–Fri. 9 AM to 5 PM Pacific Time

HELLBOY WEIRD TALES
Volume 1
ISBN 978-1-56971-622-9 | $17.99
Volume 2
ISBN 978-1-56971-953-4 | $17.99

✠

ODD JOBS
ISBN 978-1-56971-440-9 | $14.99

ODDER JOBS
With Frank Darabont, Charles de Lint,
Guillermo del Toro, and others
ISBN 978-1-59307-226-1 | $14.99

ODDEST JOBS
ISBN 978-1-59307-944-4 | $14.99

✠

B.P.R.D.: HOLLOW EARTH
By Mignola, Chris Golden,
Ryan Sook, and others
ISBN 978-1-56971-862-9 | $17.99

B.P.R.D.: THE SOUL OF VENICE
By Mignola, Mike Oeming, Guy Davis,
Scott Kolins, Geoff Johns, and others
ISBN 978-1-59307-132-5 | $17.99

B.P.R.D.: PLAGUE OF FROGS
By Mignola and Guy Davis
ISBN 978-1-59307-288-9 | $17.99

B.P.R.D.: THE DEAD
By Mignola, John Arcudi, and Guy Davis
ISBN 978-1-59307-380-0 | $17.99

B.P.R.D: THE BLACK FLAME
By Mignola, Arcudi, and Davis
ISBN 978-1-59307-550-7 | $17.99

B.P.R.D: THE UNIVERSAL MACHINE
By Mignola, Arcudi, and Davis
ISBN 978-1-59307-710-5 | $17.99

B.P.R.D: THE GARDEN OF SOULS
By Mignola, Arcudi, and Davis
ISBN 978-1-59307-882-9 | $17.99

B.P.R.D.: KILLING GROUND
By Mignola, Arcudi, and Davis
ISBN 978-1-59307-956-7 | $17.99

B.P.R.D: 1946
By Mignola, Joshua Dysart, and Paul Azaceta
ISBN 978-1-59582-191-1 | $17.99

B.P.R.D.: THE WARNING
By Mignola, Arcudi, and Davis
ISBN 978-1-59582-304-5 | $17.99

B.P.R.D.: THE BLACK GODDESS
By Mignola, Arcudi, and Davis
ISBN 978-1-59582-411-0 | $17.99

B.P.R.D.: 1947
By Mignola, Dysart, Fábio Moon, and Gabriel Bá
ISBN 978-1-59582-478-3 | $17.99

B.P.R.D.: WAR ON FROGS
By Mignola, Arcudi, Davis, and others
ISBN 978-1-59582-480-6 | $17.99

✠

ABE SAPIEN: THE DROWNING
By Mignola and Jason Shawn Alexander
ISBN 978-1-59582-185-0 | $17.99

LOBSTER JOHNSON:
THE IRON PROMETHEUS
By Mignola and Jason Armstrong
ISBN 978-1-59307-975-8 | $17.99

WITCHFINDER:
IN THE SERVICE OF ANGELS
By Mignola and Ben Stenbeck
ISBN 978-1-59582-483-7 | $17.99

DARK HORSE COMICS *drawing on your nightmares*™
darkhorse.com

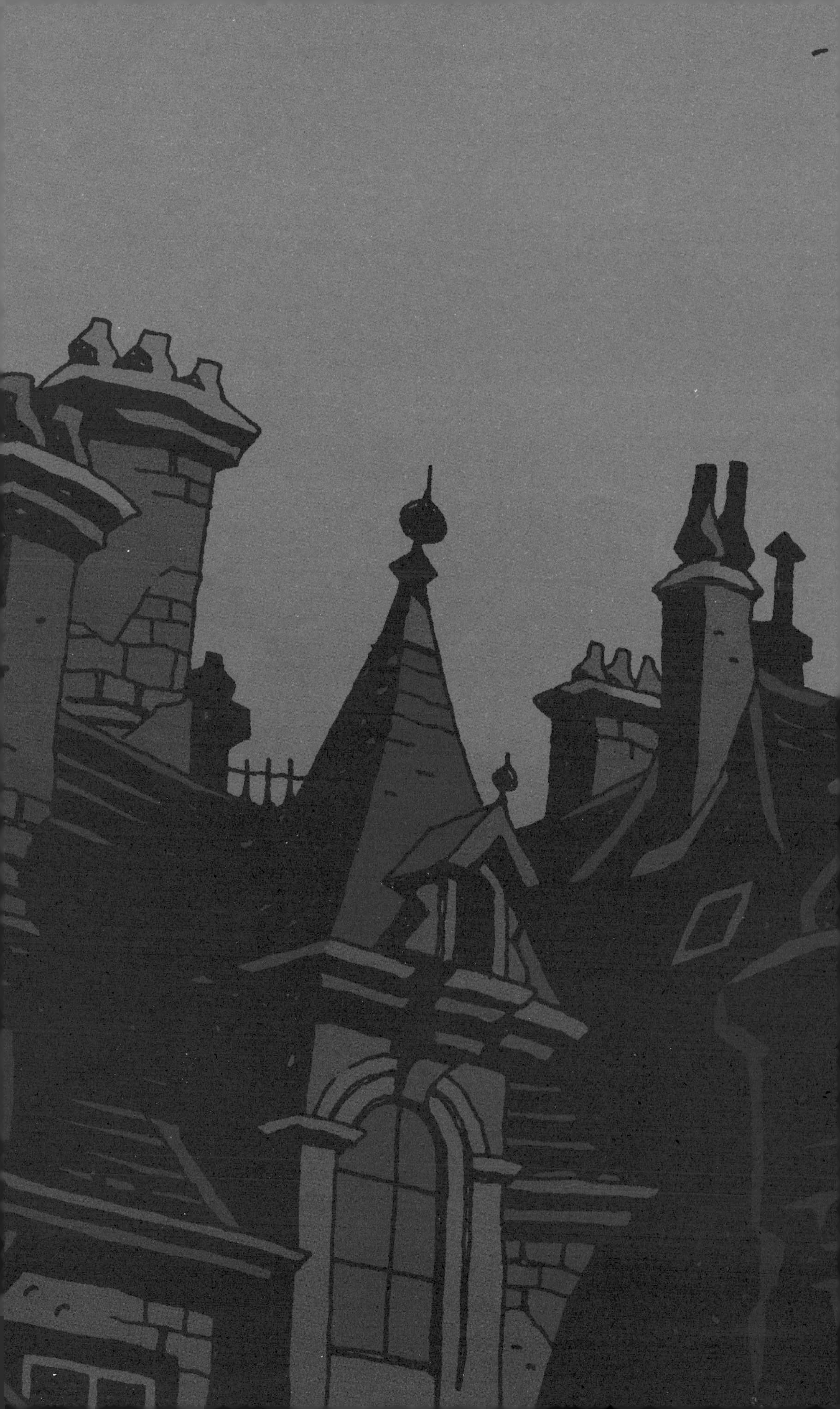